FOOD FROM THE COUNTRYSIDE

FOOD FROM THE COUNTRYSIDE

Avril Rodway

Illustrated by Zane Carey

If I should set down all the sorts of herbes that are usually gathered for Sallets I should not only speake of Garden herbes, but of many herbes, et cetera that growe wilde in the fields, or else be but weedes in a Garden; for the usuall manner with many, is to take the young buds and leaves of every thing almost that groweth, as well in the Garden as in the Fields, and put them all together, that the taste of the one may amend the relish of the other.

John Parkinson, 1629

In spring the children ate the young green from the hawthorn hedges, which they called 'bread and cheese', and sorrel leaves from the wayside, which they called 'sour grass', and in autumn there was an abundance of haws and blackberries and sloes and crab-apples for them to feast upon. There was always something to eat, and they ate, not so much because they were hungry as from habit and relish of the wild food.

Flora Thompson
Lark Rise to Candleford

Food from the Countryside

Published by Grange Books
An Imprint of Books & Toys Limited
The Grange
Grange Yard
London
SE1 2AG

ISBN 185627 276 1

First published in 1988 by
Brian Trodd Publishing House Limited
as Wild Foods.

Copyright © 1988 Regency House Publishing Limited
This edition published 1992

Printed in Singapore

For Hugh, Thomasin and Giles and
all our friends who picked and
gathered, ate, drank and commented

CONTENTS

INTRODUCTION

An interest in the wild food plants of our countryside increases the enjoyment of a ramble through woods and fields. As a solitary walker, or on a family outing, you can learn to keep an eye open for those plants which our ancestors regarded as valuable foods, but which have never, perhaps, been developed and cultivated – and add another dimension to the pleasures of the country. This book sets out to show how to use some of the commoner wild plants – but do not aim to provide your larder with large stocks of wild food all the time. Regard these foods as a welcome and interesting addition to everyday meals and remember, there are rules to follow when picking your foods from the hedgerows.

First and foremost is identification of anything you are going to eat. This book does not aim to be a botanical reference book and care should be taken, since this is a general guide only, to check any plants and fungi collected against a specialist botanical reference publication. For instance, some plants, such as members of the umbellifer family, can be very similar to each other and some are poisonous. If you are going to extend your range of fungi, you certainly need a very comprehensive and well-illustrated guide before venturing to pick and eat. The best guide of all is an experienced friend – but even then, double check with your book.

Every few years there are reports of a poisoning tragedy when someone has eaten a death cap or other lethal fungus in mistake for one that is harmless. If in doubt over *any* plant, do not pick it with cooking in mind.

Where to pick plants

You will need to keep your eyes open and will gradually learn where plants grow and thrive. There are many places to avoid. Main roads will have dusty vegetation, exposed to car exhaust fumes – so never pick there. Another hazard these days are the chemical sprays used on fields. To be on the safe side, do not pick along the edge of cultivated areas, and remember that this goes for streams and ditches, too, where water polluted with weedkillers and insecticides may have drained off the land.

The best places to look are along small country lanes, disused railway tracks (we have an extensive one in our part of the country, which has yielded a good store of wild food plants), on downs, moors, hills and in woods, by river banks and in marshes. The seashore near where I live is a good source of plant foods – here the fields and woods come down to a wide area of salt marsh, definitely gum-boot country!

I always find it a nuisance that some of the best local leafy food plants grow in a lane near our house which is a favourite walk for dogs (including our own)! This is certainly the sort of area to avoid, too, so keep an eye open if plant hunting near a village – it may not be the local Lover's Lane but Dog Walk instead.

Code of the Countryside

You would be unlikely to be reading this book if you were not a country-lover and cared for wild life, so it is probably unnecessary to remind you of the country code.

1 Take your rubbish home with you – do not throw it down to litter fields and woods.

2 Shut gates behind you.

3 Be very careful not to start fires – one cigarette end thrown down or not properly extinguished could be enough in dry weather to start a serious fire.

4 Never walk across fields containing crops, even if your map shows that there should be a path there.

5 Do not dig or pull up wild plants – unless there are special reasons, this could be illegal without the specific permission of the owner of the land. It is a measure designed primarily to protect rare species, but could apply to any wild plant.

Certain plants are protected species, others are becoming rarer – the cowslip, once so widely picked for country wines and creams, is just one example. The plants suggested here are common ones, but if you become really interested in the subject, you may want to extend your range. So check with a local or national conservation society or in a reference book if in doubt.

When you have found your plants, do not over-pick; in fact, if there are only a few specimens, it is better to leave them altogether to spread for another year. Gather a few leaves or berries from a number of plants rather than stripping one plant completely, for obvious reasons. Of course there are some plants that are very prolific, such as nettles, fat hen, dandelions and blackberries – these can be experimented with in a number of recipes, while the rarer 'finds' can add an unusual touch to just one or two dishes.

Equipment

I have got into the habit of carrying a plastic bag with me on all country walks 'just in case', but if you are going out specifically to pick wild food, it is advisable to take with you a pair of scissors, an old pair of gloves, a walking stick or umbrella with a crook end for pulling down branches and, of course, your book for identification. When blackberrying or collecting other soft berries I take a lightweight polythene bowl, because if they are collected in a plastic bag or carrier, the weighty fruit tends to go soggy.

What to pick

Most leafy plants are at their best for eating when the leaves are young, so pick them then, choosing leaves that are undamaged by insects or disease. Fruit should be ripe but not past its best and nuts full and not too green. It is best to pick in the morning when the dew has dried, but before the 'crop' has been exposed to too much sun. Try to damage the hedgerow, plants or stems as little as possible – using scissors is a great help in this. All wild food is better for being eaten as soon as possible after picking, so it pays to 'mark the spot' where the plants you want to harvest are growing, and collect them just before you are ready to cook.

Keeping a notebook will give you interest in later years. In it you can record what you picked and where, and even what recipes you used for the various plants.

What not to pick

Keep a list by you of plants *not* to eat – and add to it as your knowledge grows. The list below will start you off, but is not comprehensive.

Some plants which should **NOT** be eaten:
Aconitum anglicum (Monkshood)
Arum maculatum (Cuckoo pint)
Atropa belladonna (Deadly nightshade)
Bryonia dioica (White bryony)
Colchicum autumnale (Autumn crocus)
Conium maculatum (Hemlock)
Convallaria majalis (Lily of the Valley)
Digitalis purpurea (Foxglove)
Euonymus europaeus (Spindle tree)
Hedera helix (Ivy)
Helleborus viridis (Green hellebore)
Hyoscymus niger (Henbane)
Ilex aquifolium (Holly)
Mercurialis perennis (Dog's mercury)
Oenanthe crocata (Hemlock water dropwort)
Ranunculus (all buttercups)
Taxus baccata (Yew)
Viscum album (Mistletoe)

I have avoided giving a list of fungi, as I think these plants should not be picked at all without taking the precautions already suggested. The few I have suggested for eating are easy to identify.

Using wild foods

Different parts of plants are, of course, edible, and our country ancestors must have enjoyed a varied diet throughout the year – even in winter there are still a few leaves to be found and eaten. Whenever possible, use leaves and flowers raw in salads, sprinkled with chopped herbs and with a good dressing of oil and vinegar or lemon-juice. You can try an all-wild mixture in spring, or add wild plants to lettuce and cucumber salad. Such modest plants as chickweed, young dandelions, primroses, daisies and watercress will all add interest – and vitamins.

A number of the plants suggested in this book make very good leaf vegetables, similar to spinach. One of the best I think is fat hen, a very ancient food plant indeed, which springs up in ploughed fields, dug over gardens and even building sites. Young nettles, too, are an obvious choice. If you mention wild food, the normal reaction is always – 'Oh yes, nettle soup!' But they can be used in a number of other interesting ways – and so can dead nettles, both red and white. That bane of gardeners, ground elder, is another candidate for the cooking pot – it is a good way of taking revenge, and it has a flavour all its own.

The stems of some plants also make delicious eating. Alexanders stems, cooked like asparagus and eaten with butter, form a memorable starter – or they can be candied like angelica to enjoy as a sweetmeat or cake decoration. Hogweed stems, unlikely as they might seem, are also good, both on their own or stir-fried with other vegetables – and so are burdock stems, if picked young.

Roots are also usable. An obvious example is horseradish – and who has not heard of dandelion coffee made from the plant's root?

Look out for wild herbs. There are a number of mints, all delicious, and you may be lucky enough to find wild thyme and marjoram and, especially in coastal areas, the beautiful feathery wild fennel. Flavourings from such plants as Jack-by-the-hedge and ramsons taste mildly, but unmistakably, of garlic, and tansy or alexanders seeds used in moderation are also good.

Berries and fruits are always worth looking out for. Wild strawberries and raspberries are among the most delectable, but try too some of

Wild strawberry

the recipes for sloes, bullaces, rowan berries, crab apples, rosehips, haws and the not-to-be-despised blackberry. You may be lucky enough to live in an area where bilberries grow, with their unforgettable, rich flavour or to find a few cranberries, though these are now not common in the wild.

Fungi I have already mentioned – used with caution and prudence they can provide some flavours that are different. Seaweeds, too, repay trial and experiment. Late in the season, look for nuts, which can be used in many dishes, or simply enjoyed raw.

You will find a section of suggestions on preserving wild foods in a variety of ways – from drying to bottling, from concocting ketchups and cordials to wine-making.

All these ideas and recipes will, I hope, stimulate interest in a rewarding and fascinating hobby. Think of all these nutrients you are gaining from plants which have grown without the benefit of artificial fertilisers and which have not been polluted by chemical sprays or insecticides!

The history of the plants themselves repays research – many of them have been used for hundreds of years either for food or medicinally, and often they have interesting connections with magic or protection against the fairies or little people. Their country names can be charming, amusing – or basic. Fat hen was once known as 'muck weed' as it often grew on manure heaps; 'bumblekite' was a country name for blackberries – and, because of its known properties as a diuretic, the dandelion was called 'pissabed'!

Preserving your harvest

If you are lucky enough to find plenty of wild plants, flowers or berries to pick without feeling guilty, you may want to keep some for later use. There are many forms in which you can do this, depending on the 'crop', and you will find individual recipes under the different plant headings. Here are some general guidelines and suggestions.

Drying herbs

Make sure you pick your wild thyme, marjoram, etc on a fine morning when the plants are dry. They are at their best just before they flower.

Hang up in bunches in a warm, dry place – it can be out of doors in daytime if the weather is fine, but do not hang in full sunlight. They need not be covered, but if you like, you can make bags of cheesecloth to protect from flies and dust.

Seed heads from such plants as alexanders or fennel should be picked when the seeds are ripe and dried upside down. Shake off the seeds when completely dry and store in opaque jars, clearly labelled. I must confess to helping my alexanders seeds along in a very cool oven – they do not seem to have lost any flavour.

When your herb leaves are dry, rub or crush them lightly and store. It is important not to keep herbs in clear glass bottles or jars, as the flavour will deteriorate.

Flower heads such as meadowsweet or elderflower can be dried in the same way. Pick at their peak, when the scent is really heady, hang upside down and when dry, gently rub off the flowers from the stems.

Drying fungi

In some areas, you may discover a large stock of field mushrooms or other edible fungi – enough to make preserving them worthwhile. I have frozen mushrooms successfully – open-freeze on trays, then put into freezer bags. However, the more traditional way is to dry them, which, as in the case of dried herbs, concentrates the flavour wonderfully.

Pick over your fungi, keeping only the best specimens, and wipe to rub off any earth (do not wash them or peel). Spread out on foil and dry in a very low oven or in the sun, until they have the texture of leather. Alternatively, thread on strings and hang up in a warm dry place. When dry, store in a jar for later use.

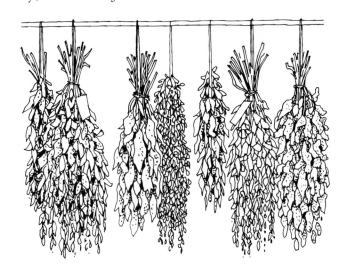

Herbs hung up to dry

Fungi drying on a sheet of foil

Drying fruit

You are more likely to have extra fruit than anything else and may want to keep it in its 'natural' form for later use as well as making jams, jellies and chutneys. The best fruits to dry are cherries, bilberries, sloes and bullaces.

Drying in the sun is appealing, if you can rely on the weather, but the fruits can just as well be dried in a low oven. They should be spread out on baking trays covered with cheese-cloth and are ready when dry but still pliable and leathery. Make sure the storage containers are really dry and are well sealed so the dried fruit will not absorb moisture and go mouldy. Pick the cherries with stalks on and do not remove stones. When dry, leave for several hours before storing.

In the case of sloes and bullaces, first scald with boiling water to split the skins and pat dry on kitchen paper. I have also dried rowan berries – as in the recipe for rowan brandy (page 112). When I came to use them, I found that another member of the family had nibbled away at them and there were very few left so that I had to dry another batch! I did not myself enjoy them in this form, but you might like to try a few and see if you acquire the same taste.

If drying these fruits appeals to you, experiment with others. Crab apples, if large enough, would be worth doing – peel, cut in half and core and thread on strings to hang above a warm stove or range, or oven dry. If you do not like the brown colour of dried apples, dip the fruit in slightly salted water when peeled and pat off excess with kitchen paper before drying. This will keep them whiter.

Below: Bottling fruit

Bottling fruit

My mother was a great fruit bottler and looking at rows of fruit stored up for winter use on the shelves of the pantry would give me a wonderful feeling of security. This is something we have now lost, to a certain extent, with the advent of the home freezer and the supermarket containing, winter and summer, a whole range of the world's produce.

You will need a supply of thick glass jars with special screw-on lids, initially expensive, but indefinitely re-usable – you may be lucky enough to find some in car boot or jumble sales; a deep pan; wooden board; trivet or some other object to stand in the pan (my mother used a dish cloth kept for the purpose); cloth or tongs with which to lift the hot jars from the pans.

Pick over your fruit, discarding any bad or damaged specimens. Make up a light syrup with a litre (2 pints) of water to 450 g (1 lb) sugar. Warm your bottles and jars and pack to the top with fruit. Depending on the fruit, press down well – you will not need to do it with such fruits as blackberries, bilberries or cranberries as they are small. Fill up the jar with hot syrup and tilt it slightly this way and that to expel any air bubbles. Screw the lids down firmly, then unscrew a fraction.

Stand the jars in the pan on cloth or trivet – it should be deep enough to allow the jars to be completely covered with water (or, in some cases, to the shoulders of the jars – see individual recipes). Fill up the pan with warm water and bring very slowly to simmering point. Simmer for 20 minutes, then remove the jars, place on the wooden board and tighten the seals. Allow to cool, before labelling.

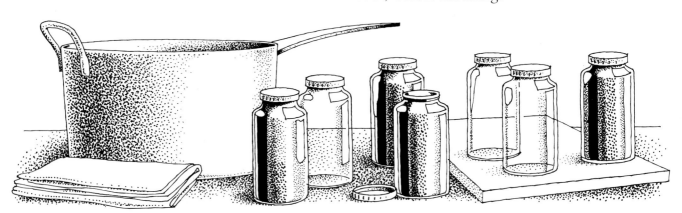

Nuts

Keep a few nuts dried for later use, but remember that birds and animals rely on them greatly for survival. Chestnuts and hazel nuts change from the green, milky flavour of the young, freshly picked nuts to the later crisp and drier texture.

Make sure nuts for storage are free from damp, and hang up in nets so that the air can circulate. The plastic net bags in which oranges are sometimes sold are worth keeping for this purpose.

Pickles, chutneys, sauces and ketchups

Pickles are slightly more tricky than chutneys. For the latter, almost anything goes and you can experiment with any spices or flavourings you like. The general principle of pickle-making is that the character of the fruit or vegetable is preserved, its flavour being enhanced by the liquid in which it is stored, which is usually sweetened vinegar or brine. Vinegar is generally a more effective preserver, brined pickles anyway being intended for more rapid consumption. However, to be on the safe side, you might like to heat process your jars of pickles for half-an-hour as in bottling fruit.

Nuts can be pickled – the classic is pickled walnuts, but you could use green hazel nuts for a change. In our part of the world, pickled samphire is greatly enjoyed. Pickling nuts is rather a complicated process, but pickling vegetables is easy. The vinegar used should be boiled up with pickling spices (crushed and tied in a bit of cheesecloth) and sugar. Any kind of vinegar can be used and any sugar – brown sugar of course gives a darker colour, as does malt vinegar.

For a crisp pickle, allow the spiced vinegar to cool before pouring into the jars, otherwise pour in hot. Some fruits and vegetables need simmering before pickling (ie crab apples or bullaces), others, like samphire, would be too limp and soft if you did this. In some recipes you will find that the vinegar needs draining off, reboiling several times and pouring over again, to give a more positive flavour.

It is important to fill the pickling jars right up and seal to make airtight as vinegar evaporates quickly. Use glass-topped jars or plastic lids – never anything metal as vinegar and metal react together and the metal quickly corrodes.

Chutney-making is much simpler, less fiddly and has fewer 'processes' on the whole than pickling. Once you have made a few chutneys from recipes you will soon be experimenting with your own. Have a range of spices in your cupboard – coriander seeds, allspice, ginger, chillies, garlic, cloves, peppercorns, nutmeg, mustard seed, mace are all suitable. The vinegar you use will affect the 'character' of your chutney, but any kind is all right, malt, cider, distilled or wine. If you do not have the exact ingredients for a recipe, do not worry. You can always substitute something else – and either white or brown sugar will do.

Basically, the fruits or vegetables are boiled up with the spices, sugar and vinegar until a thick amorphous mixture is produced. This is poured into warmed jars, covered and sealed like jam. Most chutneys improve with keeping. With a glut of fruit such as blackberries, it makes a change to use them for chutneys and sauces rather than the usual jams or jellies. One of my most popular productions is blackberry chutney.

Ketchup is useful for flavouring stews or dashing on meat or fish. Again, it is something to make when you get plenty of a suitable wild food.

Basically, the juices are extracted from elderberries, blackberries, mushrooms, etc by slow heating or long pressing. The resulting juice is cooked up with spices, sometimes with the addition of vinegar or wine, before being bottled. In some cases, to preserve the ketchup, it is necessary to heat process. If your recipe advises keeping before use, do not cheat! The flavour will undoubtedly be better.

Refreshing wild fruit sauces can make a delicious accompaniment to plain ices, custards, milk puddings, etc. Simply boil the fruit with sugar and press through a sieve. You can flavour with a little liqueur if you like – for instance, crème de menthe or apricot brandy go well with blackberry sauce – though this is not essential. If you like spicy flavours, a little of your favourite spice could go in instead. Taste and experiment at will.

Jelly making

Making jelly is great fun – mainly because you can conjure it up from any fruit to make either a sweet or a savoury concoction.

No special equipment is needed, unless you want to go to the expense of buying a special jelly bag. I use a clean cotton dish cloth, tying it up at the four corners when in use. If you do the same, be sure to wash out and rinse the dishcloth well to remove any dressing in the cloth, before using the first time.

Wild fruits make good jellies because their flavour is tart and distinctive – and I still have not finished experimenting. Sloes, blackberries, elderberries, rowan berries, haws, bilberries, bullaces are all good, to name a few. If often pays to add some chopped-up unpeeled and uncored windfall apples to the first boiling, to ensure plenty of pectin which gives a good 'set'.

The principle is simple. Just put the fruit and flavourings if used in a pan and cover with water. (Incidentally, I always use 'filtered' water in cooking as our tap supply is heavily chlorinated and without being put through a filter jug it spoils the flavour of jellies. If you do not have a filter and your water does not seem good enough, use bottled spring water – the still, not sparkling, variety.)

Bring to the boil and simmer until the fruit is soft. Put into your jelly bag or clean cloth (dipped in boiling water, then wrung out) and hang overnight to drip into a bowl. If you want a very clear jelly, do not squeeze the bag. If, like me, you do not worry too much about this, squeeze out as much juice as you possibly can to add to the bowl.

Measure the juice and to each 600 ml (1 pint) of juice add 450 g (1 lb) sugar (rather less sugar if you are making jelly for eating with meat or game). Return to pan, bring to the boil, stirring with a wooden or plastic spoon. Boil until the jelly reaches 105°C (220°F) when measured with a jam thermometer (measure in the centre of the pan). If you do not have a thermometer, spoon out a little on a saucer, cool, then see if it wrinkles when pushed with the finger. Have ready some warmed jars (I like to use a small size) and fill using a ladle. Seal with waxed paper discs and cover.

Candied fruits

Bullaces or sloes can be candied as a novelty. To candy fruits, they should first be simmered in a heavy syrup (450 g/1 lb sugar to 300 ml/½ pint water) until tender, then taken out, and left to dry on a wire tray in a cool oven. Meanwhile boil up the syrup until thick, cool a little and dip the fruit in it, using tongs or a fine skewer, until each piece is well coated. Leave to dry again before dusting with icing sugar and storing between waxed paper sheets in a box or jar.

Jams, cheeses and butters

Jams or preserves are the most common way of using fruit and consist simply of fruit and sugar brought to the boil, skimmed and simmered until a setting point is reached, when the jam is put into jars, covered and sealed. It is possible, using mixtures of wild fruits and with the addition of nuts, flavourings, etc to achieve some interesting results.

Fruit cheeses and butters are slightly different from jams. Basically, they are sugar and fruit purées cooked so long that the moisture has largely evaporated. Cheeses have more sugar in than butters and are firm when cooled, so that they can be cut – rather like blancmange. Butters, as the name implies, can be spread. Cheeses were traditionally served with whipped cream and toasted nuts, or with port after dinner. Butters were used as a spread or as a tart filling.

It takes time to make these as the fruit must be simmered slowly for a long time until it is almost dry then the sugar added. As burning is a hazard it should be stirred all the time to prevent this.

Fruit cheeses should be put to set in shallow dishes rubbed with a little oil. Seal with waxed paper, cover and keep for several months to allow the flavour to develop. Fruit butters can be put in jars and eaten as soon as you want them; I find they keep less well. Cranberries, bullaces, sloes, quinces, crab apples are all candidates for this form of preserving.

Making wine

If you have not made any wine before, you will probably want to experiment in a small way before investing in much equipment. It is a good way to use large crops of wild food such as blackberries, elderflowers, elderberries, etc and to preserve them in a very acceptable edible form! Once you get 'hooked' on country wine-making, you will no doubt experiment with your own recipes and buy a specialist book on the subject.

You will need a plastic bucket (white is best); a length of plastic tube, demi-johns or large bottles for fermentation (save up wine bottles) and smaller wine bottles for bottling, polythene bags and elastic bands, plastic sieve and wooden spoon, and a cork driver are the basics. Many large chemists sell wine-making equipment very cheaply and you can get most of your requirements, including the additives listed below, from there.

You will need something to sterilise your equipment – many wine-makers use Campden tablets, or you can buy sodium metabisulphite in powdered form. Citric acid is necessary in some form – buy it as a powder – or you can use lemons. Pectozyme is needed in some recipes to clear the wine. Some wines require tannin extract (or cold tea) and others the addition of dried fruit. Wine yeast is also necessary – either an all-purpose one or special flavour. Yeast nutrient is also helpful.

The amount of sugar you will need will vary according to whether you want a sweet or dry wine. For a dry wine 1 kg (2 lb) will be sufficient to 5 litres (1 gallon) of water. If you want a sweet wine, use more sugar.

Very generally, the method is as follows. The day before, start the yeast working by putting it in a bottle half filled with tepid water, plus a squeeze of lemon juice or a very little citric acid, some sugar and yeast nutrient. Shake well, plug the top with a twist of kitchen paper and leave in a warm place for a day. The water should be cloudy and there should be some bubbles at the top if the yeast has started to work properly.

Prepare the fruit or other ingredients as directed in the recipe. Put the fruit into the bucket. Boil up some water and leave it to cool until tepid. Add amount given in recipe to the fruit, juice, etc in the bucket, plus any additives such as lemons, dried fruit, tannin, etc. Then stir in the sugar well enough to dissolve it completely and finally add the prepared yeast mixture. Cover the bin and leave in a warm place for the time recommended, stirring well each day.

Next transfer the mixture now fermenting to your large bottles or demi-johns using a jug and funnel, first straining it from the fruit/flower sediment through a cloth into a clean bucket. Fit a special 'airlock' in each bottleneck or fix a plastic bag with a rubber band so that the bag will fill with the gases given off as if it were a balloon.

When fermentation has quite ceased and the yeast and 'bits' have settled at the bottom, siphon off the wine into the sterile bottles, being careful not to disturb the sediment. Cork the bottles using a corking gadget, and leave in a place with an even, cool temperature for the time recommended – usually not less than six months.

See individual recipes for quantities and more detailed directions.

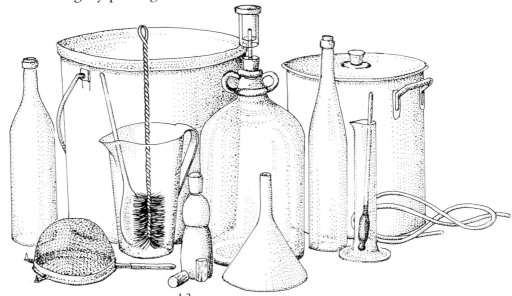

Wine-making equipment

Aegopodium podagraria

GROUND ELDER

As John Parkinson wrote in his *Earthly Paradise* (1629); 'Many herbes and flowers that have small beautie or favour to commend them, have more food use and vertue', and ground elder, introduced by the Romans, was widely cultivated then and in medieval times for use both as a vegetable and a herb of healing.

This modest-looking weed, as all gardeners know, 'cannot be admitted into gardens without great caution' or it will certainly take them over. An old name for it was gout-weed, and Nicholas Culpeper says 'It is not to be supposed that gout-wort hath its name for nothing, but upon experiment it heals the gout and sciatica; as also joint-aches and other cold pains'.

It was formerly eaten in Sweden boiled for greens, when young, and can be used in this way today. It has a distinctive flavour, which may or may not appeal to you 'neat', so you may prefer to try the recipe which includes it.

GROUND ELDER 'NATURE'
Pick the leaves when young, and as it 'boils down' considerably, allow plenty for each serving. Wash the leaves, shake but do not dry and drop into a very little boiling salted water and cover. Cook until tender, but not soggy, drain and press out the water. Add a knob of butter or margarine and 'fluff up' with a fork before serving.

MEAT LOAF WITH GROUND ELDER
450 g (1 lb) lean minced beef
50 g (2 oz) fresh wholemeal breadcrumbs
1 medium onion, finely chopped
5 g (1 tsp) dry English mustard
10 ml (2 tsp) Worcestershire sauce
5 g (1 tsp) salt
2.5 g ($\frac{1}{2}$ tsp) ground black pepper
50 g (2 oz) mushrooms, wiped and finely chopped
Large handful young ground elder leaves (about 50 g/2 oz), washed and finely chopped
2 large eggs, beaten
15 ml (1 tbsp) vegetable oil

Mix the meat, breadcrumbs, onion, mustard, Worcestershire sauce, salt and pepper, mushrooms and ground elder leaves with the egg. Lightly oil a loaf tin and pack the mixture in firmly, leaving it to 'rest' in the refrigerator for a couple of hours (or more if you like). Turn out onto an ovenproof sheet or dish and brush with the rest of the oil. Bake at 180°C/350°F (Gas 4) for an hour. Either serve hot with tomato sauce or leave to cool, chill and serve with salad.
Serves 4–6

Aegopodium podagraria

Alliaria petiolata

GARLIC MUSTARD

I prefer the sprightly name 'Jack-by-the-hedge' rather than the more staid 'garlic mustard' for this cheerful plant which does, in fact, seem to prefer hedgerows in which to flourish.

It smells and tastes of garlic, with mustardy overtones, and if cows eat it, it can give a disagreeable flavour to their milk. Remember Dairyman Crick in *Tess of the d'Urbervilles* by Thomas Hardy, whose customers complained that the butter had a 'twang'? 'The dairyman suddenly exclaimed "Tis garlic! and I thought there wasn't a blade left in that mead!"' Such was the herb's pungency that probably one bite of it by one cow had been sufficient to season the whole dairy's produce for the day! Hardy does not say whether garlic mustard or ramsons was the culprit – but either would have had the same effect on the unfortunate Mr Crick's butter.

Country people used to use it with bread and butter, salted meat and with lettuce in salads, and this gave it another name – 'sauce alone'. We can copy these uses ourselves today. Medicinally it was used for coughs and hoarseness and to strengthen the digestion.

It is not as strong as ordinary garlic, but gives a delicate flavour to such bland foods as cream cheese, eggs and sauces. It is better to use the young leaves rather than to wait until they are tough and old.

STUFFED EGG STARTER
4 large eggs
6–8 garlic mustard leaves
30 g (2 tbsp) mayonnaise
Salt and pepper to taste
Lettuce, tomato, cucumber, chopped green pepper to garnish

Hard boil, cool and peel the eggs. Cut each in half and scoop out the yolks into a bowl. Finely chop the garlic mustard leaves and mix with the egg yolks and mayonnaise, mashing all together with a fork. Taste and add more chopped leaves if you want a stronger flavour. Season. Pile the mixture back into the half whites. Arrange the salad garnish on four plates and put two half stuffed eggs on each. Serve with wholemeal bread and butter. Serves 4

SANDWICH FILLING
The same ingredients as above may be used as a sandwich filling, but in this case, chop the eggs finely and mix with the mayonnaise, garlic mustard and seasoning.

JACK-BY-THE-HEDGE'S PORK CHOPS
4 large pork chops
1 medium onion, finely chopped
150 ml (¼ pt) red wine
45–60 g (3–4 tbsp) chopped garlic mustard leaves
Salt and pepper to taste

Put the chops in a frying pan and grill on both sides until cooked. Lift out with a draining spoon and keep hot. Pour off most of the fat, leaving just a little in the pan. Add the onion and cook until soft but not brown. Pour in the wine and bring to boiling point, add the chopped garlic mustard leaves and seasoning and simmer until the liquid is reduced to about half. Put the chops in a serving dish and pour a little of the sauce over each. Serve with plain boiled potatoes and a salad. Serves 4
Note: Use chopped garlic mustard in oil and vinegar dressing in place of garlic.

16

Alliaria petiolata

RAMSONS

Woodland garlic, with its dark green leaves and starry white flowers, grows in woods throughout Europe and quite widely in the British Isles. You certainly can not ignore it if you come across a 'garlic wood' – the smell is all-pervasive. If used raw, you will need only a little of the chopped leaves in salad dressings or in salads, but when cooked, the flavour tends to fade, so those who like their garlic strong will need to use a fair quantity.

RAMSONS SALAD
1 crisp lettuce (Webb's or Cos)
8 rashers streaky bacon
2 ripe avocados
3 or 4 ramsons leaves, to taste
Oil and vinegar dressing

Rinse, dry and shred the lettuce and place in a large bowl. Grill the bacon, cool and chop. Halve the avocados and remove the stones; take out the flesh and cut into cubes. Finely chop the ramsons leaves. Put the bacon, avocados and ramsons in the bowl with the lettuce, pour over dressing to taste and lightly toss together. With chunks of new bread and butter this makes a good light lunch dish, or starter for a more substantial meal.
Serves 4

TABOULI WITH RAMSONS
175 g (6 oz) bulgur
100 g (4 oz) parsley
15 g (1 tbsp) chopped chives or onion
2 large tomatoes
3 or 4 ramsons leaves
For the dressing:
15 ml (1 tbsp) white wine vinegar or lemon juice,
     15 ml (1 tbsp) vegetable oil, pinch dry mustard, pinch sugar, salt and pepper

Soak the bulgur overnight in water. Drain very well, pressing out all the water with the back of a spoon. Finely chop the parsley and ramsons, skin and chop the tomatoes and blend together the ingredients for the dressing. Mix all the ingredients together and taste, adding more ramsons or seasoning if necessary. Chill. Serve garnished with olives and with hot pitta bread.
Serves 4
(Note: Bulgur (or burghul) is cracked wheat and is obtainable from supermarkets or health food shops.)

Allium ursinum

Arctium minus

BURDOCK

Burdock is probably best known for its prickly burrs which children love to throw at one another and which stick so firmly to clothes (and hair!). A bizarre use for the burrs which I came across in an old book runs as follows: 'Boys catch bats by throwing the prickly heads up into the air'. It is widely found in Japan, where the roots are commonly eaten.

If you want to use burdock as a food plant, you will need to pick the stems young (before the flowers occur) and scrape off the outer rind. When I was a child, we used to drink dandelion and burdock, a rather bitter and very black concoction which I did not like very much, made of the roots of both plants. However, try the recipe for yourself. The roots should be dug early in the year, so you will need to identify the plant during the summer and mark the place where it grows.

STEM STARTER
8 15-cm (6-in) lengths of young burdock stem per person
Melted butter

Wash the young stems and scrape off the outer covering. Tie in bundles and drop into boiling salted water, cooking until tender (or steam, if preferred). Serve hot with melted butter – or cold, if you like, with vinaigrette dressing.

BURDOCK AND DANDELION
2 medium burdock roots
Equivalent weight of dandelion roots
4.5 litres (1 gallon) water
550 g (1¼ lb) soft dark brown sugar
1 large lemon
25 g (1 oz) brewer's yeast

Dig the burdock roots when the plants are just beginning to sprout, wash thoroughly and chop up. Weigh and add the equivalent of cleaned, chopped dandelion roots. Put them to boil in about half the water for 15 or 20 minutes, then add the sugar and juice of the lemon. Stir until the sugar has dissolved, strain into a clean bucket and add the rest of the water. When tepid, sprinkle the yeast on top and leave in a warm place to ferment for three or four days. When the ferment has subsided, bottle in screw-top bottles and leave for at least a week before drinking. Inspect and let out a little of the 'fizz' if it seems to be too frothy.

Other uses for burdock: The stems can be candied – see recipe for candied alexanders stems (see page 110). Use young burdock leaves in salad – but they must be *very* young. The young stems, scraped, may also be eaten raw.

Armoracia rusticana

HORSERADISH

Horseradish flourishes almost anywhere and on a hot summer day you can often smell its unmistakable pungent aroma from where it is growing on waste land, a railway embankment or the side of a field. It is so widespread that it seems hardly worth growing it specially, although if you plant it in prepared ground and care for it you will obtain straighter and probably longer roots. The leaves are very large and dock-like and it has imposing spikes of small white flowers. The root is the part used.

It originated in eastern Europe and has been widely used for many centuries, at first as a medicine, and later in sauces. One former use was as a face-wash, the scraped root being infused in cold milk, though my cynical source, an early 19th-century writer, remarks 'that after all it would probably be of more real service if taken into the stomach instead of being daubed about the face'! Judging by the effect that scraping it has on one's eyes, the facewash idea is not very appealing! It was also recommended as an inhalant by some physicians to cure bad colds – an obvious example of the remedy being more uncomfortable than the disease! In fact, peeling and grating horseradish is a job best done in the garden or by an open window.

You will not be able to pull up horseradish – its roots are strong and tough – so take a spade to dig it up with. Wash the root and peel or scrape off the outer layer. A little freshly grated or shaved onto roast beef is very nice – but do it as you are about to have the meal as it quickly loses its pungency. Alternatively, preserve or use it in one of the sauces, pickles or recipes given below.

HOT HORSERADISH CREAM

50 g (2 oz) butter or margarine
25 g (1 oz) plain flour
450 ml ($\frac{3}{4}$ pt) milk or milk and single cream mixed
30 g (2 tbsp) horseradish, grated
5 ml (1 tsp) vinegar
1.25 g ($\frac{1}{4}$ tsp) salt
2.5 g ($\frac{1}{2}$ tsp) sugar

Melt the butter in a pan and add the flour, blending well. Heat the milk and gradually add to the butter and flour, off the heat, stirring continuously. Put back on the heat and cook, stirring for 5 minutes or until the mixture thickens. Add the horseradish, vinegar, salt and sugar and mix together. Serve hot with fish or roast meat.

COLD HORSERADISH SAUCE

Yolks of 2 large hard-boiled eggs
75 ml (5 tbsp) white wine vinegar
25 g (1 oz) horseradish, grated
2.5 g ($\frac{1}{2}$ tsp) salt
5 g (1 tsp) caster sugar
15 ml (1 tbsp) single cream

Put the egg yolks into a basin, crush and work them with a spoon until smooth. Gradually add the vinegar and stir until the mixture becomes creamy. Add the other ingredients in order, stirring well together. Serve with cold meat, cold smoked mackerel, etc.

HORSERADISH VINEGAR

100 g (4 oz) grated horseradish
7.5 g (½ tbsp) shallots, finely chopped
2.5 g (½ tsp) salt
1.25 g (¼ tsp) cayenne pepper
1 litre (2 pt) malt vinegar

Mix together the horseradish, shallots, salt and cayenne. Boil the vinegar and pour over the horseradish mixture, cover and leave in a warm (but not hot) place for 10 days. Strain into a pan, bring to the boil, cool and bottle. Store in a cool dry place.

PICKLED HORSERADISH

Horseradish, peeled and cut into 1.2 cm (½ in) lengths may be simply pickled to use as required by packing in wide-necked jars, covering with malt vinegar and corking. Should be stored in a cool, dry place.

RUSTIC CHICKEN

4 chicken pieces, or one 1.4 kg (3 lb) chicken cut into four
Salt and pepper to taste
50 g (2 oz) butter or margarine
225 g (8 oz) button mushrooms
1 large onion
2.5 g (½ tsp) dried thyme or marjoram
1 clove garlic
90 ml (6 tbsp) dry white wine
150 ml (¼ pt) double cream
20 g (1 heaped tbsp) horseradish, freshly grated
50 g (2 oz) white grapes, peeled, de-seeded and halved

Wipe the chicken pieces and season with salt and pepper. Melt the butter in a pan and brown the chicken pieces all over then transfer them to a baking dish and put in the oven, at 190°C/375°F (Gas 5) and cook for 50–60 minutes or until tender.

Pour off most of the fat from the pan in which the chicken was cooked and add the wiped and trimmed mushrooms, onion, chopped finely, the thyme or marjoram and the crushed garlic.

Pour in the wine and stir round, simmering until reduced. Add the cream, bring to the boil, turn down the heat and simmer for a few minutes. Then add the horseradish, correct the seasoning, and add the grapes. Heat through when ready to serve and pour it over the chicken which you have arranged on a heated serving dish. Serve with rice and a green salad.
Serves 4

HORSERADISH SHEPHERD'S PIE

900 g (2 lb) lean minced beef
1 onion, chopped
1 clove garlic (optional)
5 g (1 tsp) mixed herbs
15 g (1 tbsp) flour
300 ml (½ pt) strong beer or stout
30 g (2 tbsp) horseradish, grated
30 ml (2 tbsp) malt vinegar
Tomato slices
675 g (1½ lb) cooked potatoes, mashed, with a little milk and seasoning, or made-up instant mash
Knob butter or margarine

Put the beef into a pan over a medium heat and brown, stirring and breaking up the meat. Add the onion, the crushed garlic and the herbs.

When the meat is browned and the fat running, stir in the flour and continue cooking for a minute or two until the flour is blended in. Gradually add the beer or stout and bring to simmering point. Cover and cook on a low heat for about 15 minutes, checking that it is not burning and add a little water if the mixture is getting too solid.

While the meat is cooking, soak the horseradish in the vinegar and at the end of cooking time, add both to the beef mixture with salt and pepper to taste. Put in a piedish or casserole and spread with the thinly-sliced tomatoes then with the mashed potato. Pattern the top with a fork and dot with butter.

Put in the oven at 180°C/350°F (Gas 4) for 20–30 minutes until the meat is completely cooked and the top of the pie browned. Serve with a green vegetable.
Serves 6

FISH ARMORACIA

1 kg (2.2 lb) firm white fish such as brill or hake
300 ml ($\frac{1}{2}$ pt) white wine vinegar
1 large onion
2 stalks celery
1 medium leek
1 bayleaf
1.25 g ($\frac{1}{4}$ tsp) mixed herbs
Salted water or stock
For the sauce
1 large cooking apple
30 g (2 tbsp) horseradish, grated
5 ml (1 tsp) honey
Salt and pepper

Skin fish and remove bones and cut the flesh into small strips. Put in a saucepan and cover with the vinegar. Bring to the boil, skim and drain, reserving the vinegar.

Clean and cut the onion, celery and leek into thin pieces. Heat a small quantity of salted water (or better still fish stock, made from the fish trimmings) with the herbs and add the vegetables. Cook until nearly tender, then add the fish and continue simmering until all are cooked. Drain, and keep hot.

Peel the apple and grate it. Mix with the horseradish and honey (melted in a little water) and add enough of the fishy vinegar to form a smooth sauce. Spread over the fish and vegetable mixture and heat all through in a moderate oven. Serve with plain boiled rice or boiled new potatoes. (Or serve alone as a starter)
Serves 4

GALLIANO PARTY DIP

300 ml ($\frac{1}{2}$ pt) soured cream
100 g (4 oz) full fat soft cheese
5 g (1 tsp) dry mustard
15 g (1 tbsp) grated horseradish
25 ml (1 fl oz) Galliano
Salt and pepper
30 g (2 tbsp) chopped chives or green part of
    spring onions

Combine the cream, cheese, mustard and horseradish with the Galliano and mix well. Taste and add salt and pepper and a little more horseradish if you prefer a stronger flavour. Fold in half the chives or onion tops. Cover and leave in the refrigerator for at least four hours.

Serve sprinkled with the remaining chives or onion, with savoury biscuits, vegetable sticks or cubes of cheese to dip in.

Horseradish

Castanea sativa

SWEET CHESTNUT

Do not confuse the sweet chestnut tree with the horse chestnut, whose nuts are inedible, though full of interest for children playing 'conkers'. The trees are not, in fact, related and the leaf form is quite different. The nut husks of the sweet chestnut are covered with fine sharp spines close together, rather like a sea urchin's shell, while horse chestnut husks, although they have some spines, are largely smooth. In certain parts of Europe chestnuts were not only boiled and roasted, but made into puddings, cakes and bread and one has only to drive through the Cevennes in France during the autumn to see how widely grown the trees still are.

'They are reckoned a very flatulent and indigestive diet', remarks one old medical book, 'although in Italy there are instances of men's living to the age of eighty, and even a hundred years, who have fed wholly upon chestnuts.' Longevity-producing or not, it is fun to gather a basket of ripe chestnuts in a good year, bring them home and roast them on an open fire (or failing a fire, in the oven). After taking the ripe nuts from their husks be sure to 'nick' the skins with a knife before roasting, or they will be popping all over the place! An old country 'game' I have seen quoted was to give a name to each chestnut sitting roasting in a row by the fire. The first nut to 'pop' was the first lover who would ask you to marry him – if you try this, you will have to leave the chestnut skins uncut, of course.

Roasting is the simple way to eat sweet chestnuts, but they can be used in all manner of recipes, savoury or sweet. Traditionally they are used in poultry stuffing – or try them boiled and mixed with sprouts for a novel winter vegetable. A handful added to the pot gives interest to almost any stew or casserole.

VEGETARIAN BAKED CHESTNUTS
450 g (1 lb) chestnuts
1 medium onion, finely chopped
1 clove garlic, finely chopped
25 g (1 oz) parsley, chopped
5 g (1 tsp) dried mixed herbs
About 300 ml ($\frac{1}{2}$ pt) white sauce made with 15 g ($\frac{1}{2}$ oz) butter, 15 g ($\frac{1}{2}$ oz) flour and 300 ml ($\frac{1}{2}$ pt) milk
Salt and pepper to taste
40 g (1$\frac{1}{2}$ oz) wholemeal breadcrumbs
25 g (1 oz) butter

Slit and roast or bake the chestnuts until cooked. Boil in a little water until very tender, then rub through a sieve or process (include the water). Mix with the onion, garlic, parsley and herbs, then with the white sauce. Season to taste. Put in an ovenproof dish, sprinkle the breadcrumbs on top and dot with the butter. Bake at 190°C/375°F (Gas 5) until firm and brown (about 30–40 minutes) and serve with a salad or sprouts.

Castenea sativa

SPROUT AND CHESTNUT SOUP

225 g (8 oz) chestnuts, weighed after roasting and
    shelling
225 g (8 oz) sprouts, trimmed
2 stalks celery, chopped
Small onion, chopped
1 litre (2 pt) chicken stock
600 ml (1 pt) milk or milk and water (approx.)
Salt and pepper

Simmer the chestnuts, sprouts, celery and onion
in the stock until very tender. Blend or press
through a sieve. Thin with the milk and water
until creamy in consistency. Check seasoning
and if liked stir in 15 ml (1 tbsp) sherry and 15 ml
of cream. Serve with croûtons or wholemeal
rolls.
Serves 4–6

CHESTNUT SAUCE

300 ml ($\frac{1}{2}$ pt) stock
150 ml ($\frac{1}{4}$ pt) single cream (or milk and cornflour
    – see below)
225 g (8 oz) chestnuts
Strip of lemon rind
Cayenne pepper
Salt

Nick the chestnut skins and roast or bake them
for about 20 minutes. Remove the skins and put
nuts in a pan with the stock and lemon rind.
Simmer until tender (about 30 minutes). Remove
rind, blend or rub chestnuts and stock through a
sieve, add cayenne and salt and re-heat. Stir in
the cream and use as required. If using milk, mix
with 8 g (1 heaped tsp) cornflour and stir into the
purée when hot, simmer for 5 minutes. Season
with a pinch of cayenne and salt. Use this sauce
to re-heat cold turkey or chicken.

CANDIED CHESTNUTS

900 g (2 lb) chestnuts
300 ml ($\frac{1}{2}$ pt) water
450 g (1 lb) sugar

Bake and skin the chestnuts as above. Boil in
water until tender. Cool and drain. Boil 300 ml
($\frac{1}{2}$ pt) water with the sugar to form a thick syrup,
then dip the chestnuts in on the end of a skewer
and place on an oiled plate to dry. Dust with
icing sugar and store between layers of greaseproof paper. Do not keep long before eating.

CHESTNUT ICE IN-A-BASKET

For the ice cream
300 ml ($\frac{1}{2}$ pt) double cream
25 g (1 oz) icing sugar
15 ml (1 tbsp) Drambuie or brandy
100 g (4 oz) chestnut purée (see method on page
    27) sweetened with 25 g (1 oz) sugar
For the baskets
50 g (2 oz) butter
30 ml (2 tbsp) golden syrup
50 g (2 oz) caster sugar
50 g (2 oz) plain flour
2.5 g ($\frac{1}{2}$ tsp) ground ginger
Grated chocolate or chocolate vermicelli and
    whipped cream to decorate.

Make the ice cream as follows. Whip the cream
until fairly, but not too, stiff. Stir in the icing
sugar, Drambuie and chestnut purée. Mix well,
then freeze until semi-solid. Beat well, then
smooth the mixture and put back in the freezer to
harden.
    To make the baskets, preheat the oven to
150°C/325°F (Gas 3). Lightly grease two baking
trays, then melt butter, syrup and sugar in a pan.
Remove from heat, cool for two minutes then
mix in the flour and ginger. Place teaspoons of
the mixture on the trays 7.5 cm (3 in) apart. Bake
for about 15 minutes until light brown and full of
holes. Remove from the oven, cool slightly then
lay each in turn round the base of an upturned
glass jar so they harden in a basket shape. (It is
tricky to get the baskets of a uniform size –
experiment is needed before offering to guests!).
When cool, store in a tin until ready for use. To
serve, fill each with a scoop of ice cream and
decorate with a little whipped cream and grated
chocolate. This is very rich so a small quantity is
sufficient.
Serves 6–8

CHESTNUT QUEEN PUDDING

225 g (8 oz) chestnuts
1 small lemon
300 ml ($\frac{1}{2}$ pt) milk
50 g (2 oz) fresh white breadcrumbs
25 g (1 oz) butter
25 g (1 oz) caster sugar
2 large eggs
15 g (1 tbsp) caster sugar
Vanilla essence
Strawberry jam
Sugar

Nick the chestnut skins and roast or bake until cooked. Remove skins. Put into a pan and just cover with water. Simmer until tender, then blend or put through a sieve. Meanwhile, simmer the thinly cut lemon rind in the milk for 15 or 20 minutes and strain it over the breadcrumbs. Cream the butter and 25 g of sugar until smooth, add the egg yolks, the juice of the lemon and a few drops of vanilla essence and stir in the chestnuts, breadcrumbs and milk. Put into an ovenproof dish and bake at 190°C/375°F (Gas 5) for 20 to 30 minutes, until the mixture is firm and brown. When cooled a little, spread thinly with strawberry jam. Whip the egg whites until stiff, fold in 10 g (2 tsp) of sugar, pile onto the pudding and sprinkle with more sugar. Turn down the oven heat to low (120°C/250°F/G$\frac{1}{2}$) and bake until meringue is set. Serve with single cream.
Serves 4

CHESTNUT SOUFFLÉ PUDDING

150 g (6 oz) chestnuts weighed after cooking and
   removal of skins
25 g (1 oz) plain chocolate
300 ml ($\frac{1}{2}$ pt) milk
25 g (1 oz) butter
25 g (1 oz) flour
50 g (2 oz) cake crumbs
4 medium eggs
50 g (2 oz) sugar
2.5 ml ($\frac{1}{2}$ tsp) vanilla essence

Put chestnuts into a pan with water barely to cover, cook until very tender, drain and blend or put through a sieve. Break up the chocolate and simmer in the milk until dissolved. In another pan, melt the butter, stir in the flour and cook for two or three minutes, then stir in the milk and chocolate mixture and stir until it boils. Add the cake crumbs and stir and cook until the mixture leaves the sides of the pan. Cool then beat in the egg yolks, sugar, chestnut purée and vanilla essence. Beat the egg whites until stiff and stir into the mixture. Pour into small buttered moulds and bake at 190°C/375°F (Gas 5) for 30 to 40 minutes until risen and set but still moist inside. (Alternatively cook in a large dish but in this case cook longer – up to an hour). Serve at once on its own or with cream.
Serves 6–8

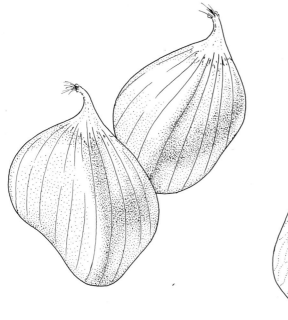
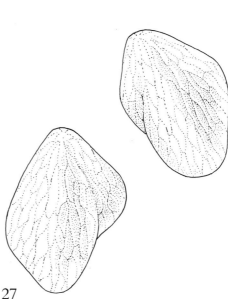

FAT HEN

Fat hen is so common and ordinary in appearance, springing up as it does at the edges of fields, in waste land, on building sites and in forgotten corners of the garden, that it is easy to underestimate it. According to Thomas Green's *Universal Herbal* of 1820 'it occurs in every garden, on every dunghill and in almost every corn field. It is mentioned by several authors as being boiled and eaten for greens, and is known by the name of fat hen or muck-weed. Linnaeus affirms that swine are extremely fond of it.' In fact, it is one of the most delicious of the leafy food plants and it and its close relations, the goose-foot family, oraches, Good King Henry, and so on have been eaten by man for many hundreds of years.

Its seeds formed part of the last ritual meal eaten by the Bog People (Tollund Man), whose preserved bodies have been found in the peat bogs of Denmark, and the American Indians are also said to have enjoyed it in large quantities, baking the seeds to use as grain. Its place is now taken by spinach, but up to recent times, in periods of war or famine, men have been glad to eat it again. Rightly so, as it is said to contain more protein and iron than either cabbage or spinach.

Of all edible weeds, its name is the one which always catches the imagination and makes people smile. Tell them they are eating fat hen, and they will go away and talk about it afterwards with interest and amusement. How did it come by it?

The only explanation I have seen is that it was derived from the German *Fette Henne*, as it was originally used in Germany for feeding poultry – in other words, it was a 'hen fattener'! Its beautiful Anglo-Saxon name was 'melde', and this is retained in several place names in the British Isles.

If you happen to live in Buenos Aires, Pennsylvania or New Jersey, however, the *Universal Herbal* warns against Chenopodium anthelminticum or Worm-seed goosefoot which, it remarks, 'has a disagreeable scent, and the seeds are given to chickens against the worms'!

In the recipes suggested, you can use fat hen, any of the goosefoot or oraches singly or together. It 'cooks down' in the same way as spinach, so you will need to gather a good quantity to make a serving. When the plant is young and tender, you can use it stems, flowers and all. When it has grown up, use the side shoots, leaves and seeds only as the stems will be too tough.

To serve as a vegetable accompaniment to meat dishes, wash the fat hen well and do not drain. Put a little water and salt in a pan with the fat hen, bring to the boil and cook for one or two minutes only. Drain very well, chop and add a little butter (and perhaps 15 ml (1 tbsp) cream or top of the milk if you want extra richness). Taste and correct seasoning – I like mine with a tiny pinch of nutmeg, but this is just a personal preference you might like to try for a change.

Chenopodium album

VEGETABLES WITH FAT HEN SAUCE

900 g (2 lb) broad beans
225 g (8 oz) young carrots
225 g (8 oz) fat hen
45 ml (3 tbsp) single cream
Salt and pepper to taste

Shell beans, scrape carrots and cut into rings. Drop into boiling salted water and cook until tender. Meanwhile, cook the fat hen in a small amount of salt water. When tender, press out all the water, add the cream and seasonings and blend to a smooth sauce (if too thick, add a little more cream). Reheat, pour over the hot vegetables, turn with a spoon and serve. Serves 4–6

AVOCADO DIP WITH FAT HEN

2 large, ripe avocados
10 ml (2 tsp) lemon juice
30 ml (2 tbsp) single cream
1 large clove garlic, crushed
10 ml (2 tsp) brandy
100 g (4 oz) fat hen
Salt and pepper to taste

Skin the avocados and remove the stones. Blend together the avocados, lemon juice, cream, garlic and brandy. Cook the fat hen until very tender in a little salted water and drain very well. Blend fat hen into rest of mixture. Season to taste. Serve with crisps as a dip, or as a starter with toast.

CHILLED SUMMER SOUP

450 g (1 lb) frozen peas (or the same quantity of fresh shelled peas)
1 medium onion
40 g ($1\frac{1}{2}$ oz) butter or margarine
Large handful fat hen leaves, chopped
850 ml ($1\frac{1}{2}$ pt) chicken stock
1.25 g ($\frac{1}{4}$ tsp) nutmeg
Salt and pepper
15 g (1 tbsp) chopped mint
5 g (1 tsp) sugar
15 ml (1 tbsp) double cream

Defrost the peas. Chop onion finely. Melt the butter in a pan and add the onion and fat hen leaves and 'sweat' together for 8–10 minutes, stirring occasionally, but otherwise leaving covered. Then pour in the stock (which you can make from stock cubes and water if you do not have any homemade stock), the peas, nutmeg and salt and pepper. Bring to just below boiling point and simmer until the peas are tender. Cool slightly and blend or press through a sieve. Add the chopped mint and sugar and check the seasoning. Leave to chill in the refrigerator (this can be overnight if you like) and serve with a swirl of cream in each bowl and French bread and butter. Serves 4

FAT HEN NUT PÂTÉ

225 g (8 oz) cooked, mashed potato
225 g (8 oz) mixed minced nuts (eg almonds, walnuts, unsalted peanuts)
15 g (1 tbsp) sesame seeds, toasted or plain
15 ml (1 tbsp) tomato purée
2 eggs, beaten
5 g (1 tsp) each fresh mint and lovage (or other herbs) finely chopped
15 ml (1 tbsp) mushroom ketchup
2 cloves garlic, crushed
15 ml (1 tbsp) vegetable oil
450 g (1 lb) fat hen

Mix together all the ingredients except the fat hen. Cook the fat hen in a little boiling salt water until tender, drain, press out all the water and chop. Put half the nut mixture into a loaf tin, spread the cold fat hen on top, then press in the rest of the mixture. Put in the refrigerator to chill. Turn out and decorate with slices of cucumber and radish roses. Serves 4–6

GOOSEBERRY SAUCE FOR MACKEREL

225 g (8 oz) gooseberries
100 g (4 oz) fat hen
25 g (1 oz) butter
25 g (1 oz) sugar (more if you prefer a sweeter sauce)
2.5 g ($\frac{1}{2}$ tsp) nutmeg
10 g (2 tsp) chopped chives
2.5 ml ($\frac{1}{2}$ tsp) lemon juice
Salt and pepper

Boil the gooseberries in a little water until very tender. Drain. Cook fat hen in boiling salt water until soft, drain well. Mix together the gooseberries, fat hen, butter, sugar, nutmeg, chives and lemon juice and blend into a smooth sauce. Taste and adjust seasoning. Reheat before serving.

Chondus crispus

CARRAGHEEN or IRISH MOSS

Although its name suggests it is a localised plant, this common seaweed is found round many coasts and is rich in vegetable gelatine. In fact, it can be used in place of ordinary gelatine and made into jellies, blancmanges or to thicken soups and stews. It should be gathered in spring to find it at its best, as seaweed, like all plants, has its seasons. At this stage, its flat stem and branching fan-like fronds will be a light brown – look out for it growing on rocky shores.

It can be used fresh, or if you can spare the time and effort, dried by first washing and then spreading it out of doors so that it is alternately dried and washed by the rain (give a helping hand in dry weather by pouring water over it from time to time). When it has turned white it is ready for storage. Trim off the tough bits and store in bags or jars. Use as if it were fresh. Carragheen was formerly administered as a dose for sore throats or gland troubles and it contains iodine and other valuable salts.

Try one of the recipes as a novelty – it may be cooked either with water or milk. Mrs Beeton recommends it as a nourishing drink for invalids, and no doubt the addition of wine or brandy she adds to the basic mixture of carragheen, sugar, lemon juice and water would do its part!

MRS. BEETON'S CARRAGHEEN CHOCOLATE
25 g (1 oz) fresh or reconstituted dried carragheen
25 g (1 oz) plain chocolate, grated
Sugar to taste
600 ml (1 pt) milk

Put the carragheen in a pan with 600 ml (1 pt) of water and bring to the boil. Heat the milk nearly to boiling point, add the chocolate and stir until dissolved. Add the water strained from the moss and sweeten to taste. Serve hot, in warmed glasses, with a little extra chocolate grated on top.

To make a nutritious blancmange, follow the above procedure, but be sure to press out all the gelatine from the carragheen when straining the water into the milk, to give a good set. Cool and leave in the refrigerator until firm and decorate with piped cream and more grated chocolate.
Serves 4

GINGER LEMON JELLY
25 g (1 oz) fresh or reconstituted dried carragheen
600 ml (1 pt) water
45 ml (3 tbsp) sweet sherry
Juice of $\frac{1}{2}$ lemon
30–45 g (2–3 tbsp) sugar, to taste
5-cm (2-in) piece fresh ginger root

Soak the cleaned carragheen for two hours in cold water. Drain. Put it and the peeled and chopped ginger root and other ingredients in a pan with 600 ml (1 pt) water and simmer gently for about an hour, adding more water as evaporation occurs to keep the liquid quantity the same. (For a stronger lemon flavour, add the half lemon shell to the mixture for about half the cooking time.) Strain into a mould, pressing well to extract all the gelatine. Leave in the refrigerator until set.
Serves 4

Chrysanthemum (or Tanacetum) vulgare

TANSY

This beautiful plant has dark green, ferny leaves and flat groups of small, buttonlike, bright yellow flowers. The leaves are very aromatic and their flavour is strong, so use them sparingly.

Tansy derives its name from the Greek *athanaton*, meaning 'deathless' and the fact it was once used in embalming may account for this. So too may the fact that the flower heads are 'everlasting'.

In the past tansy was a great cure-all, and was often used in gipsy medicine. It was said that its juice aids conception – a belief based on the fact that it flourishes where that most prolific animal the rabbit abounds!

A 'tansy' was a kind of pudding formerly eaten at Easter, partly as a reminder of the bitter herbs eaten at the Passover and partly, one suspects, as a blood purifier at the end of winter when green vegetables had been scarce. The chopped leaves can be used as a flavouring for omelettes, pancakes, soups and puddings – but keep tasting and trying – it is easy to overdo this pungent herbal addition. In large doses it can be an irritant and have a narcotic effect.

OLD-FASHIONED TANSY PUDDING
600 ml (1 pt) milk
25 g (1 oz) butter
150 g (6 oz) fresh white breadcrumbs
50 g (2 oz) ground almonds
50 g (2 oz) sugar
30 ml (2 tbsp) rosehip syrup
Grated rind of 1 small lemon
7.5 g (½ tbsp) tansy leaves, finely chopped
4 eggs

Heat together the milk and the butter just to boiling point. Pour over the breadcrumbs, stir and leave to soak for an hour. Mix in the ground almonds, sugar, syrup, lemon and tansy leaves. Beat the eggs, mix into the breadcrumbs mixture and pour into a greased dish. Bake at 180°C/350°F (Gas 4) for 60 to 80 minutes until set. Serve with whipped cream.
Serves 4–6

PORK KEBABS
For the marinade
15 g (1 tbsp) tansy leaves, finely chopped
10 ml (2 tsp) honey
30 ml (2 tbsp) dry cider
5 g (1 tsp) mustard powder
15 ml (1 tbsp) vegetable oil
For the kebabs
1 medium onion
8 button mushrooms
4 small tomatoes
450 g (1 lb) diced lean pork

Combine the marinade ingredients in a large bowl. Peel the onion, divide into pieces and blanch in boiling water for a few minutes. Wipe the mushrooms. Put pork, onion, tomatoes and mushrooms into the marinade and leave for an hour (or longer if time), stirring occasionally. Thread the ingredients alternately on kebab skewers, having halved the tomatoes. Brush with a little vegetable oil. Grill, turning, until pork is tender. Serve with rice and lettuce and dandelion leaf or other salad.
Serves 4

Chrysanthemum vulgare

Corylus avellana

HAZEL

Delicious hazelnuts (or filberts as the cultivated form are called), are well worth collecting late in the year. The nuts are encased in a leafy covering and you can pick or buy them with this still on. At this stage, the kernels are milky and sweet and best eaten just as they are, dipped in a few grains of salt. Later, when ripe, the nuts in their shells are crisper and drier. The bush itself is quite unremarkable during the summer, but in spring, the male flower appears in the form of a 'lamb's tail' catkin while the female flower, which produces the nuts, is a tiny red and almost invisible bloom.

All nuts stored in the shell should be in a dry, warm place, with plenty of air circulating. String bags are ideal – save those in which you can sometimes buy oranges and re-use them.

The nutritional value of hazelnuts is high and, as Mrs Beeton remarks, 'they are very free from oil and disagree with few persons'. Certainly they are versatile and make a very acceptable addition to salads, muesli, nut loaves and fresh fruit mixtures.

HAZELNUT OPEN SANDWICHES
Butter some brown bread. Chop up 30–60 g (2–4 tbsp) of hazelnuts and mix with a little mayonnaise to bind. Spread on the bread and sprinkle with paprika. Trim off the crusts and cut into triangles. Serve garnished with mustard and cress.

Nux avellana, hazel nut

HAZELNUT AND CHEESE SAVOURY

25 g (1 oz) grated Cheddar (or similar) cheese
25 g (1 oz) grated Parmesan cheese
50 g (2 oz) shelled hazelnuts
1.25 ml ($\frac{1}{4}$ tsp) made mustard
Pinch cayenne pepper
295 g (10.4 oz) tin condensed consommé
200 ml (7 fl oz) double cream
Milk
Watercress to decorate

Mix the cheeses in a bowl, add chopped nuts, mustard and cayenne pepper. Beat the consommé, which should have been chilled for at least 4 hours in the refrigerator, with a whisk or hand blender. Mix with the cheeses. Whip the cream and add to the mixture. Now add sufficient milk, a little at a time, until the mixture is creamy. Pour into four or six ramekins, depending on size, and leave to set. Garnish with watercress and serve with toast or crispbread as a starter or savoury. (If you wish to make this for vegetarians, make up a vegetable consommé using 150 ml ($\frac{1}{4}$ pt) water, half a vegetable stock cube and an envelope of gelatine. Leave to set and use as the consommé).
Serves 4–6

HAZELNUT CRUMB CAKE

50 g (2 oz) white breadcrumbs
30 ml (2 tbsp) rum or sweet sherry
150 g (5 oz) sugar
5 medium eggs
150 g (5 oz) hazelnuts, finely chopped
300 ml ($\frac{1}{2}$ pt) double cream

Dry the breadcrumbs in a low oven until crisp but not browned, and mix with 15 ml (1 tbsp) of the rum. Separate the eggs and whisk the yolks and sugar together in a double boiler over hot water until the mixture is thick and creamy. Whisk the egg whites until stiff and dry. Fold the breadcrumbs, nuts and whites into the yolks, mixing very lightly but until completely blended. Put into a greased and floured 20-cm (8-in) cake tin and bake at 190°C/375°F (Gas 5) for 45 to 60 minutes or until a skewer pushed into the centre comes out clean. Turn out and cool. When cold, split and sandwich together with the cream which you have whipped and mixed with the rest of the rum or sherry.
Serves 4–6

HAZEL AND CELERY MAYONNAISE

3 stalks of celery
50 g (2 oz) hazelnut kernels
30 ml (2 tbsp) mayonnaise
15 ml (1 tbsp) whipping cream
Salt and pepper

Finely chop the celery and hazelnuts, season to taste. Gradually add the mayonnaise, whip the cream stiffly and add this too. Pile in a bowl and decorate with radish roses and chopped parsley or watercress. Use as a pleasant garnish for cold roast chicken or game.

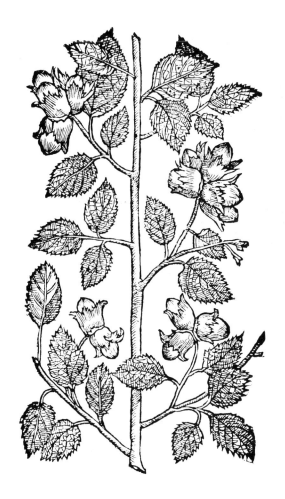

Corylus sylvestris, wild hedge nut

Crambe maritima

SEA KALE

You will be lucky to find this plant (its old name is sea colewort) in any great quantity nowadays in the wild, but you might come across it along sandy or shingle beaches. In its budding form, and from its leaves, sea kale looks very like broccoli, and the flowers when they come out are yellowish.

If there is plenty you might try a little – it is best if the young spring stems are covered with shingle or sand and are thus blanched. The flowerheads too can be eaten, when they are still in bud. If there is only a small amount, do leave it to grow.

It is sometimes possible to buy sea kale in exclusive greengrocers' shops – or you might get such a taste for it that you want to cultivate it yourself. But it will take three years before you can cut it and, like asparagus, it needs careful growing.

BLANCHED SEA KALE STARTER
Allow about 100 g (4 oz) for each serving. Trim off the root, wash and tie in bundles with fine string. Drop into boiling salted water and cook until tender when tested with a skewer. Drain and serve hot with melted butter.

FLOWER BUDS
Pick the buds, trimming off the tougher parts of the stem. Cook in boiling salt water until tender but still crisp and serve with butter or white sauce to which you have added a sprinkling of nutmeg.

Crambe maritima, sea kale

Crataegus monogyna

HAWTHORN

The hawthorn is one of the 'plants of power' of the ancients and the 'oak, ash and thorn' were a potent trio. In Ireland lone self-sown 'fairy thorns' are still regarded today as belonging to the 'little people'. I met an Irish woman only a few months ago who told me that her family have one on their farm and regularly put bread and milk beneath it for the fairies. On no account will the superstitious fell, prune or transplant such a tree – there are too many stories of accidents and ill-luck befalling the person who has done such a deed.

The Holy Thorn (one of the crataegus family) at Glastonbury in the west of England, which legend has it, sprang from the staff of Joseph of Arimathea, blooms in winter – on Christmas Day, or near it – and cuttings from it flourish in both Britain and America. In fact, reverence for the hawthorn has crossed the Atlantic and many of the same feelings for the tree exist in both Britain and the United States.

The flowers of the hawthorn, or May blossom, have a heavy, heady scent, and this used to be connected with illness and death in past ages. My Victorian-born grandmother would never allow hawthorn blossom to be brought into the house, and I can still remember wilting bunches I had gathered sitting in jamjars outside on the window sill. However, the strongly protective nature of the tree caused it to be used to shield houses against lightning and the influence of bad fairies.

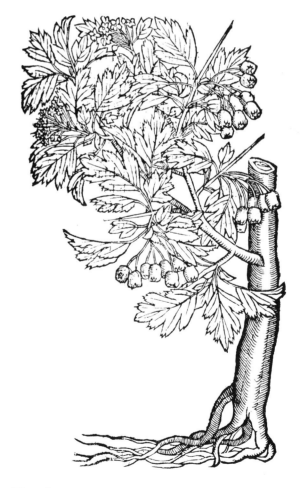

Hawthorn tree

37

Be that as it may, the hawthorn is a handsome tree in every stage, and all its leaves, flowers and berries may be used in cooking. Hungry country children are used to nibbling the nutty-flavoured buds which are commonly called 'bread and cheese'. It is such a common and prolific flower that we need not feel too guilty about picking it.

Putting paid to the apparent nonsense of the old nursery rhyme 'here we go gathering nuts in May', I have seen it suggested that for 'nuts' we should read 'knots', as the flower clusters were then known.

A crusading knight would give a sprig of hawthorn tied with pink ribbon as a token that he 'lived in hope'.

BUD AND BACON PUDDING
For the pastry
200 g (8 oz) self-raising flour
5 g (1 tsp) salt
100 g (4 oz) shredded beef suet
Water to mix
For the filling
50 g (2 oz) young hawthorn buds
3 rashers streaky bacon

Sift the flour and salt into a bowl. Mix suet with some of the flour and chop until fine, then add rest of the flour and mix thoroughly. Add 90–105 ml (6–7 tbsp) of water and mix to a soft dough. Knead lightly until smooth, then roll out thinly on a floured board into an oblong shape. Cover with the buds, pressing them lightly in (if you need a few more to cover, add them). Cut the de-rinded bacon rashers up very finely and spread over the buds. Damp the crust edges with water and roll up as for jam roly-poly. Wrap in greaseproof paper and steam for 1–1½ hours until cooked. Serve with a rich brown gravy.
Serves 4

HAWTHORN SALAD
450 g (1 lb) cooked potatoes
45 ml (3 tbsp) mayonnaise
Salt and pepper
45 g (3 tbsp) hawthorn buds

Dice the potatoes while still warm and mix with the mayonnaise. Season to taste, and when cool, add the hawthorn buds. Fold in well and chill before serving.

HAW CURD
450 g (1 lb) haws
450 g (1 lb) cooking apples
45 ml (3 tbsp) fresh grapefruit juice plus the grated rind of one grapefruit
300 ml (½ pt) water
225 g (8 oz) sugar
100 g (4 oz) butter
2 eggs

Have ready some small jars, washed in boiling water and placed in a low oven to dry.

Cook the haws in the water with the apples, grapefruit juice and rind until soft and pulpy (the apples should be cut up, but there is no need to peel or core them). Press through a sieve and return to a clean pan. Put back on a low heat, add the sugar and butter and stir until dissolved. Beat the eggs lightly and gradually add to the pan, stirring all the time and being careful the mixture does not boil. When incorporated and the mixture has thickened, ladle into the heated jars, cover and label. This is not a 'keeper' and should be eaten within two or three weeks unless stored in a refrigerator when it will keep a little longer.

FLOWER LIQUEUR
May blossom
Brandy
Sugar

Pick the flowers when the scent is strongest and the blossoms are dry. Snip off the flowers, leaving the stems, and pack loosely into a wide-necked jar. Cover with brandy and add a little sugar (about 15 g (1 tbsp) to 300 ml/½ pint). Put in a warm place out of the light and turn occasionally for a few weeks to mix the sugar. Then leave undisturbed for three to four months. Strain carefully into a clean bottle and cork firmly. It is now ready to use.

Crataegus monogyna

Fagus sylvatica

BEECH

It is included in a long list of trees quoted by the Welsh bard Taliesin as being used by the ancient Celtic gods of light to overcome the gods of darkness. Its wood was used for very many purposes ranging from furniture, farm implements, wheels, baskets and wedges to shipbuilding and musical instruments.

Caesar remarked that the beech was not growing in Britain when he visited it, but it has since been cultivated all over the country for hundreds of years. Beech leaves were formerly used in mattresses and the nuts dried and powdered to make bread, roasted for coffee or even pressed (in poor parts of Europe) to give oil.

In the early part of the 18th century an inventive economist called Aaron Hill set up a project for paying off the national debt with the oil of beech nuts, but in northern countries they were found to yield so little oil that the idea had to be dropped!

It is one of the most handsome of the forest trees – fine in form and beautiful in colour, from the young pale green leaves of spring to the russet of its mast and autumnal foliage. Its botanical name 'fagus' comes from a Greek word signifying to eat – probably referring to the early use of its mast or nuts as a food for the common people or for feeding pigs.

LEAF SANDWICHES
Use very young beech leaves in brown bread sandwiches. Chop up the leaves finely, spread the bread slices thinly with butter and cream cheese, then with the leaves and a squeeze of lemon juice. Top with another slice of bread and serve cut into triangles.

LEAF NOYAU
Young beech leaves
Gin
Sugar
Brandy
Almonds

Take a wide-necked jar and fill it loosely with young, lightly crushed beech leaves. Fill up with gin and leave, covered, for a week. Remove the old leaves and put in fresh leaves. Cover and leave for a week again. For each 600 ml (1 pt) gin, make a syrup with sugar in the proportion of 450 g (1 lb) sugar to 300 ml ($\frac{1}{2}$ pt) boiling water (stir until the sugar is dissolved). Mix the syrup and gin with 10 ml (2 tsp) brandy. Bottle when cold, and to each bottle add 3 or 4 almonds, shelled but not blanched. Use in various recipes (see below).

Fagus sylvatica

FLOSTER

1 sherry glass of sherry
½ sherry glass of noyau
15 g (½ oz) lump sugar
3 thin slices lemon
1 small bottle soda water
Ice

Mix all the ingredients together in a large tumbler and drink through a straw.
Serves 1

NOYAU ICE CREAM

600 ml (1 pt) half-frozen lemon water ice
½ sherry glass noyau
Juice of 1 orange
300 ml (½ pt) whipping cream
10 g (2 tsp) caster sugar

Beat together the water ice, noyau and orange juice, place in a container and freeze until beginning to become stiff. Beat again and refreeze. Beat together the whipping cream and sugar until stiff. Ladle portions of the ice cream into individual glasses and top with the whipped cream.
Serve at once.
Serves 4

BACCHUS CUP
½ bottle champagne (or dry sparkling white wine)
300 ml (½ pt) sherry
75 ml (⅛ pt) brandy
1 liqueur glass noyau
15 g (1 tbsp) caster sugar
Few leaves lemon balm, crushed
1 large bottle soda water
Ice

Put the champagne, sherry, brandy, noyau, sugar and balm into a large jug, mix well, let it stand for a few minutes then add the soda water and ice and serve at once.

HOT NUT DRINK
Beech nuts
Milk
Sugar to taste

Not every year is good for beech nuts – or 'mast'. Sometimes the shells do not fill out and are not worth the sorting and picking. However, in a good year, shell as many nuts as you have patience for and dry them in a hot oven until brittle. Grind and use as you would coffee, serving black or with milk and sugar to taste.

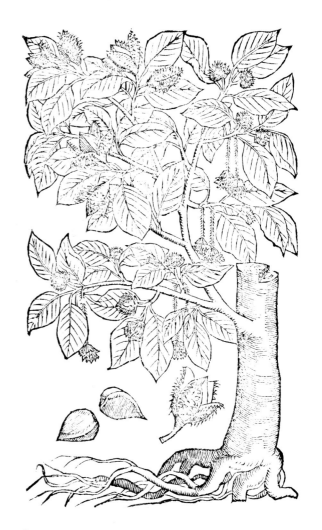

Beech

42

Filipendula ulmaria

MEADOWSWEET

I must confess that meadowsweet is one of my favourite wild food plants on three counts – its beauty, perfume and delicious flavouring for food and drinks. It grows in damp, marshy places, and the flowers fill the air with a spicy fragrance. The leaves are also aromatic and were used in past ages to flavour mead and other drinks. Old herbals liken the taste of the leaves when chewed to orange-flower water, and say that when an infusion of the flowers is added to mead it gives it the flavour of the Greek wines.

Meadowsweet was a sacred herb to the Druids, and was one of the favourite strewing herbs of Queen Elizabeth I. She 'did more desire it than any other herb to strew her chambers withal', presumably because of its delicious fragrance. As the herbalist Gerard remarked 'The smell thereof makes the heart merrie and joyful and delighteth the senses'.

MEADOWSWEET CORDIAL
6 or 8 heads meadowsweet flowers
180 ml (12 tbsp) water
180 g (12 tbsp) sugar
2 lemons

Put all the ingredients in a pan, having grated off the lemon zest and squeezed the juice. Bring to the boil, simmer for 8–10 minutes, then strain into a bottle, cool and cork. Use diluted in the proportion of 30 ml (2 tbsp) cordial in a glass, filled up with soda and crushed ice – or use with gin and soda. It is best kept in a refrigerator.

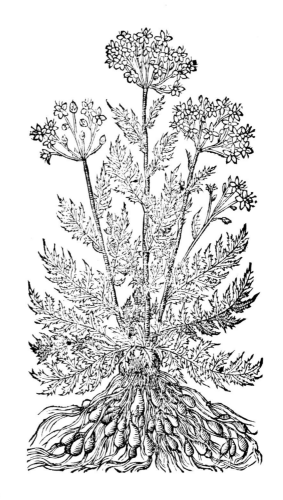

Filipendula, dropwort

PERFUMED APERITIF
Bottle sweet white wine
4 heads meadowsweet flowers
2 leaves meadowsweet, crushed

Open the bottle of wine, pour into a jug and add the flowers and leaves. Leave at room temperature for 3 or 4 hours, then chill slightly, strain and serve.

MEADOWSWEET AND BANANA MOULD
90 ml (6 tbsp) hot syrup made from 100 g (4 oz) sugar, 300 ml (½ pt) water and 6 meadowsweet heads (boil together until syrup is scented, strain)
15 g (1 tbsp) gelatine
150 ml (¼ pt) single cream
225 g (¼ lb) mashed bananas
5 ml (1 tsp) lemon juice

Below right: *Filipendula angustiflora*, narrow-leaved dropwort
Below: *Filipendula montana*, mountain dropwort

Mix the gelatine into the hot syrup. Mash or blend cream, bananas and lemon juice together. Mix with the gelatine mixture, pour into a wetted mould and leave to set in the refrigerator. Un-mould and decorate with whipped cream and chopped walnuts.
Serves 4

PEACH AND MEADOWSWEET WATER ICE
3 large ripe peaches
1 large orange
120 ml (8 tbsp) cold meadowsweet sugar syrup (see previous recipe)
White of 2 eggs

Peel and remove stones from peaches. Purée or sieve the flesh, add orange zest and juice and the meadowsweet syrup. Freeze until beginning to set, then beat thoroughly. Stiffly whip the egg whites, fold into the peach mixture and re-freeze until required. Serve with sponge finger biscuits.
Serves 4

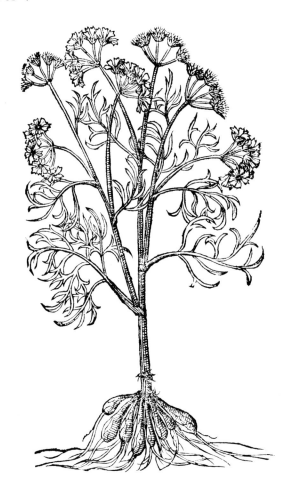

Filipendula ulmaria

FENNEL

Wild fennel, along cliffs and in hedgerows, is an attractive and showy plant, putting up heads of yellow flowers held on stems covered with feathery foliage.

Traditionally used with fish, the leaves, stems and seeds can all be used for cooking. Fennel also plays a part in the nine-herbs charm, which dates from Saxon times:

'Thyme and Fennel, a pair great in power,
The Wise Lord, holy in heaven,
Wrought these herbs while He hung on the cross;
He placed and put them in the seven worlds to aid all, poor and rich.'

CRISP CABBAGE SALAD
750 g (1½ lb) white cabbage
1 medium onion
30 ml (2 tbsp) white wine vinegar
45 ml (3 tbsp) vegetable oil
5 g (1 tsp) fennel seeds

Finely slice the cabbage and finely chop the onion. Mix oil and vinegar together and stir in the fennel seeds. Pour oil mixture over the cabbage and onion in a bowl, stir well and chill before serving.
Serves 6–8

FISH AND FENNEL PARCELS
4 cod steaks
25 g (1 oz) butter
2.5 g (½ tsp) fennel seeds or 10 g (2 tsp) chopped fennel leaves

Wash the fish and pat dry on kitchen paper. Lay the steaks on a piece of foil and dot with the butter and sprinkle with fennel. Fold the foil over to make a parcel, then bake at 180°C/350°F (Gas 4) for half-an-hour or longer, until the fish is cooked. (The advantage of this dish is that you can cook it for longer at a lower heat, or for a shorter time at a higher heat as you wish. The fennel butter gives a delightful flavour to the fish.) Unfold the foil and place fish on a warmed serving dish, spooning the fennel butter over. Garnish with lemon wedges and serve with sauté potatoes and peas.
Serves 4

RICH FENNEL SAUCE
300 ml (½ pt) whipping or double cream
5 ml (1 tsp) thin honey
15 ml (1 tbsp) lemon juice
45 g (3 tbsp) fennel leaves, finely chopped
Salt and pepper

Whip the cream until thick, but not too stiff. Stir in the honey and lemon, then the fennel. Season and blend well together. Serve chilled. Make this in summer when the fennel is in leaf – it is the perfect sauce to go with cold trout or cold fresh salmon.

FISH FILLETS WITH FENNEL SAUCE
8 fillets of plaice
125 g (4 oz) butter
1 medium onion
185 g (6 oz) mushrooms
Salt and pepper
150 ml ($\frac{1}{4}$ pt) soured cream
1.25 ml ($\frac{1}{4}$ tsp) Tabasco sauce
2.5 g ($\frac{1}{2}$ tsp) fennel seeds
15 g (1 tbsp) fresh chopped fennel leaves to garnish (if available)

Grill the fillets, dotted with the butter, under a hot grill until cooked, remove fillets and keep warm.

Peel and thinly slice the onion and mushrooms. Put the onions in the pan with the butter in which the fish was cooked, cook until transparent over a low heat, then add the mushrooms and cook for another 2–3 minutes. Season with salt and pepper, then add the cream, Tabasco sauce and fennel seeds. Heat together gently until the sauce is hot but not boiling, then pour over the fish. Sprinkle with the fennel leaves if available – if not, use chopped parsley or chives. Serve with grilled tomatoes and plain boiled potatoes.
Serves 4

BREAD WITH FENNEL
300 ml (1 pt) water
15 g (1 tbsp) dried yeast
5 g (1 tsp) sugar
5 g (1 tsp) salt
450 g (1 lb) plain flour
5 g (1 tsp) fennel seeds (more if liked)

Warm the water and mix the yeast and sugar with half of it. Set aside in a warm place until frothy. Sift salt and flour together and add the fennel seeds. Pour the yeast liquid into a well in the middle and mix. Then add enough of the

Common fennel

remaining warm water to form a dough.

Put dough on a floured board and knead for 10 minutes. Oil a large polythene bag and put the dough inside. Leave in a warm place until it has doubled in size. 'Knock' the dough down and divide it, shaping it into two round loaves. Leave to rise again. Pre-heat the oven to 220°C/450°F (Gas 8).

When the dough has risen again, put on an oiled baking sheet and place in the oven. Bake for 10 minutes, then lower the temperature to 210°C/425°F (Gas 7) and cook for a further 20 to 30 minutes or until the bread is baked. (It should make a hollow sound when tapped underneath). Leave to cool.

If after testing the loaf for flavour you find the fennel taste too strong or too weak, next time adjust the amount of seeds you use.

Fragaria vesca

WILD STRAWBERRY

The name 'strawberry' arose because the running stems of the plant are strewed (or 'strawed') over the ground, not because they are often bedded on straw to keep them clean. You are lucky indeed if you can find a patch growing wild – and it is well worth planting some in a border or strawberry pot in the garden. The flavour is absolutely superb, and when you have once tasted wild strawberries it makes you realise how much has been lost in the larger but insipid berries bought in a shop.

Even if you can find only a few, they are well worth eking out using some of the recipes in this section. If you can get a good picking, there is no better way to enjoy them than with a squeeze of orange juice, a little sugar and lightly whipped cream, though you might like to try some of the recipes, too, which call for larger quantities.

In the past, strawberries were highly regarded as not only do they 'dissolve the tartarous incrustations upon the teeth', but they also 'impart a violet scent to the urine and promote perspiration'. The old herbal I am quoting continues rather archly, 'It would be unpardonable not to inform our fair readers that they have likewise the credit of being a cosmetic or beautifier of the skin.'

If you want to grow wild strawberries, a Victorian gardening book advises that 'the wood strawberry is best, when the plants are taken fresh from the woods, provided they be taken from fruitful plants, because they are not so liable to ramble and spread as those which have been long cultivated in gardens'. Even earlier, in the 16th century, Thomas Tusser in *Five Hundred Points of Good Husbandry*, suggests the same thing:

'Wife, into thy garden, and set me a plot
With strawberry roots the best to be got:
Such growing abroade among thornes in the wood,
Well chosen and picked prove excellent food.'
Shakespeare has this to say about strawberry cultivation in *Henry V*:
'The strawberry grows underneath the nettle,
and wholesome berries thrive and ripen
best neighbour'd by fruit of baser quality.'
These days, of course, those of us who are concerned for the countryside will not want to dig up wild plants. However, wild strawberry seeds can now be obtained from specialist nurseries, or you may be lucky enough to have a friend who can supply you with some runners

WILD STRAWBERRY FRITTERS
For the batter
50 g (2 oz) plain flour
Pinch salt
Yolks of 2 eggs
30 ml (2 tbsp) double cream
30 ml (2 tbsp) water
White of 1 egg
225 g ($\frac{1}{2}$ lb) wild strawberries

Sift flour and salt into a basin, then add the egg yolks, cream and water gradually to form a smooth batter. Leave in the refrigerator for at least an hour, then stir in the stiffly whipped egg white and the strawberries. Have some hot oil ready and place tablespoons of the mixture in it. Cook until golden-brown. As the fritters are ready, drain on absorbent kitchen paper and keep hot. Serve sprinkled with caster sugar.
Serves 4

Fragaria vesca

STRAWBERRY CARAMEL

450 g (1 lb) wild strawberries
300 ml ($\frac{1}{2}$ pt) double cream
Demerara sugar

Put the strawberries into an ovenproof dish which is pretty enough to serve from. Whip the cream until very stiff and spread over the strawberries. Cover with a layer of sugar at least 3-mm ($\frac{1}{8}$-in) deep – the amount of sugar you need varies according to the diameter of the dish you use. Heat the grill until very hot and slip the dish under a few minutes before you want to serve the caramel. When the sugar is dark brown and bubbling, but not burnt, take out and serve immediately (or leave until cold to serve).
Serves 4–6

FRAGRANT SYLLABUB

150 g (6 oz) ripe wild strawberries
Medium or sweet white wine
15 g (1 tbsp) caster sugar
300 ml ($\frac{1}{2}$ pt) double cream

Crush the strawberries with a fork and add enough wine to make up to 200 ml ($\frac{1}{3}$ pt). Stir in the sugar until dissolved. Whip the cream until it stands in stiff peaks and mix with the strawberries. Divide the strawberry mixture between four goblets and leave in the refrigerator for half a day so that some of the wine separates out at the bottom of the glasses.
Serves 2–4

WILD STRAWBERRY CREAM

450 g (1 lb) wild strawberries
300 ml ($\frac{1}{2}$ pt) double cream
1 packet gelatine made up with hot water as instructions
Juice of 1 lemon
75 g (3 oz) caster sugar

Blend the strawberries to a fine purée. Whip the cream until stiff. Mix together the strawberries and cream. Dissolve the sugar in the gelatine and add lemon juice. Mix all the ingredients together thoroughly, pour into a mould and leave to set in the refrigerator.
Serves 4

STRAWBERRY SHORTBREAD

100 g (4 oz) butter or margarine
100 g (4 oz) caster sugar
Yolk of 1 egg
15 ml (1 tbsp) sweet sherry
150 g (6 oz) plain flour
Pinch of salt
25 g (1 oz) cornflour

Blend together the butter and sugar until smooth and creamy then beat in the egg and sherry. Add the flour, salt and cornflour, stir together and work until a pliable mixture is formed. Form into two equal rounds and mark one out into eight with a knife, pricking all over and fluting edge. Lightly grease a baking tray and place the short-bread rounds on it, allowing room for a little spreading. Bake at 180°C/350°F (Gas 4) until pale brown and crisp. Allow to cool.

For the filling
300 ml ($\frac{1}{2}$ pt) double cream
100 g (4 oz) ripe wild strawberries
Caster sugar

Whip the cream until stiff. Add the strawberries and a sprinkling of caster sugar. Spread the strawberries and cream on the plain shortbread round, then place the marked round on top. Sprinkle with caster sugar and serve.
Serves 6–8

WILD STRAWBERRY FLAN

450 g (1 lb) wild strawberries or wild and culti-vated strawberries mixed
Caster sugar
Whites of 2 eggs
15-cm (6-in) cooked flan case, bought or home-made

Pile the prepared strawberries in the flan case, mounting them in the centre, and dredge with caster sugar. Stiffly beat the egg whites, add 10 g (2 tsp) sugar, beat again and pile over the fruit. Again dredge with sugar. Put in the oven and bake at a low heat – 120°C/250°F (Gas $\frac{1}{2}$) – until meringue is set (60–80 minutes). Serve cold with cream. Serves 4

ASH

Together with oak and thorn, the ash was thought to protect against evil influences. An early 19th-century writer remarks that 'It is probably owing to the remains of Gothic veneration for this tree that the country people in the south-east part of the kingdom (Great Britain) split young ashes and pass their distempered children through the chasm, in hopes of a cure. They have also the superstitious custom of boring a hole in an ash and fastening in a shrew-mouse. A few strokes with a branch of this tree is then accounted a sovereign remedy against cramps and lameness in cattle, which are ignorantly supposed to proceed from this harmless animal. In many parts of the Highlands of Scotland at the birth of a child, the midwife puts one end of a green stick of this tree into the fire, and while it is burning, receives into a spoon the sap which oozes out of the other end and administers this as the first spoonful of liquor to the new-born babe.'

On a more practical note, the same writer observes that 'the ash has no equal for drying herrings!' and 'the leaves have been gathered to mix with tea and poor people in some places have made a considerable advantage by collecting them for this purpose'.

ASH KEY PICKLE
Young ash keys
Vinegar boiled with spices in the proportion of 600 ml (1 pt) malt vinegar to 25 g (1 oz) mixed cloves, black peppercorns, coriander seeds, mustard seeds and allspice; small piece fresh ginger root; 2 cloves garlic, pinch chilli powder; 15 g (1 tbsp) brown sugar

Pick the ash keys off the stems and boil until tender, changing the water two or three times to get rid of any bitter flavour. While they are boiling, bruise the pickling spices, peel and chop the ginger root and garlic and boil all up together with the sugar, chilli powder and vinegar in an aluminium pan. Have ready a warmed jar. Drain the ash keys and pack in while still hot, then pour over them the boiling vinegar (this can have the spices removed or not, as you prefer). Seal carefully with a non-metallic lid or covering. It is important to pick only very young and tender ash keys – the pickling solution can be your own favourite rather than the ingredients above.

FRENETTE
This curiosity is one you will probably only want to try if you are interested in herbal health remedies as it is said to be 'tonic, stomachic, diuretic, laxative, refreshing and sudorific'! The recipe is French and quoted by Jean Palaiseul in *Grandmother's Secrets*, published by Hutchinson and now in the Penguin Handbooks series.

Take 90 g (4 oz) roasted chicory and pour boiling water over it. Dissolve 3 kg (6½ lb) sugar and 45 g (2 oz) tartaric acid in several litres of boiling water. Moisten 60 g (2½ oz) ash leaves, picked in summer and dried in shade, with boiling water – leave to infuse for two hours and strain. Pour all three preparations into a 60 litre (approx 8 gallon) container and add more water (but not to the top). When cool enough, add 50 g (2 oz) yeast mixed with cold water. Ferment for 11 days, bottle and keep for at least 15 days, firmly corked, before drinking.

FUNGI

When the Moon is at the full
Mushrooms you may freely pull;
But when the moon is on the wane,
Wait before you pluck again.
(Essex saying)

Of all Anglo-Saxon attitudes, caution over eating fungi is one of the most widespread – and it is one I share. As I have said elsewhere in this book, it is essential to buy a really good and well-illustrated reference book if you become interested in trying out different types of edible fungi – and if in the slightest doubt about any specimen, *do not eat it*. Remember, death from mushroom poisoning is even older than the Romans. I have chosen four types of fungus which are easier to recognise than most and the descriptions are as exact as I can make them.

Agaricus campestris   FIELD MUSHROOM
Even this most common of fungi *can* be confused with other species and you must make sure that the specimens you pick have all the characteristics of a true field mushroom. You are likely to find it in autumn in fields, old pastures or old lawns and it sometimes occurs in rings. It is not usually under trees or in woods. The top of the mushroom is mainly white but can develop a brown scaly patch in the centre as it grows older. The gills underneath are close together and turn from pink in young specimens to brown later. The stem is solid and white and the ring round the stem, left when the cap has opened, disappears quite quickly thereafter. Very importantly, there is never any yellow in the flesh or bright yellowing at the base of the stem when cut, which is characteristic of *Agaricus xanthodermus*, similar to the field mushroom, but poisonous. The latter also has a prominent ring and a peculiar smell rather like ink.

Coprinus comatus   SHAGGY INK CAP
Another name for this attractive fungus is Lawyer's Wig and once you have seen it with its curly white or brownish scales, you will understand why. It grows in clusters in grass, fields or at roadsides and often pops up where ground has been dug over. You will find it in every season except winter, though I have picked it most commonly in the autumn. It is cylindrical in its young form, with a white, pink or buff stem and the young gills are white, turning through pink to black in old, open specimens. Collect it young for eating, having identified it by watching one or two of its brothers go through all the stages of growth. It has a most delicious mild flavour and attractive form and needs little cooking as the flesh is very delicate.

Lepiota procera   PARASOL MUSHROOM
These large, dramatic and handsome mushrooms are very similar when young to shaggy parasols (*Lepiota rhacodes*) and both species grow in groups by the edge of roads or woods and in fields. The caps are brown at first and, when open, turn into brown scales on a lighter background, the shaggy parasol, as its name suggests, having more curly or flaky scales. Stems of both are very tall but the ordinary parasol is taller than the shaggy one. The ordinary parasol has a brown flecked stem with two whitish rings while that of the shaggy parasol is a plain beige. Another way of telling the difference is that the flesh of the shaggy parasol turns to a reddy-brown colour when cut. The flavour is very good and one parasol mushroom is ample for one serving.

Lepiota procera, parasol mushroom

Lycoperdon perlatum   PUFF BALL
There are several species of puff ball which are edible, including the dramatic giant puff ball (*Lycoperdon giganteum*) which I have never been lucky enough to find, although I did once bring one back from a delicatessen in Amsterdam. The main thing to remember about your small puff balls is to eat them young, as when they become older the white flesh inside, which resembles cream cheese in appearance, becomes powdery and dark brown and the spores burst out through a small hole at the top. Puff balls vary from a round to a pear shape and sometimes are covered with tiny spines, though other varieties are smooth. If in doubt, cut your puff ball in half to check that its interior is smooth and white. It is sometimes possible to confuse puff balls with earth balls of which there are many varieties (botanical name, *Sclerodermatales*). These have a root-like structure at the bottom, unlike the puff balls, which only spring from one tiny, unob-trusive point. The mature earth balls have an olive colour within when cut and they do not let go their spores from a single orifice, but the whole of the ball decays. In some areas earth balls are eaten, in others they are regarded as poison-ous – so if in doubt, do not!

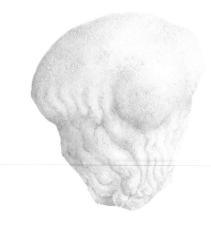

Lycoperdon perlatum, puff ball

Agaricus campestris, field mushroom

FIELD HARVEST SUPPER
450 g (1 lb) field mushrooms
1 large onion
5 g (1 tsp) chopped thyme
2.5 g ($\frac{1}{2}$ tsp) garlic or onion salt
2.5 g ($\frac{1}{2}$ tsp) ground black pepper
300 ml ($\frac{1}{2}$ pt) dry cider
4 eggs, hard-boiled and shelled
Cornflour

Pre-heat oven to 180°C/350°F (Gas 4). Peel and slice mushrooms thickly and chop the onion finely. Put all the ingredients (except cornflour) into a casserole, stir well and cook covered for 20 minutes. Stir a little of the liquid from the casserole into 10 g (2 tsp) of cornflour, stir the mixture into the casserole and put back in the oven for 5 to 10 minutes or until the liquid thickens. Serve with hot French bread and butter.
Serves 4

FIELD MUSHROOMS GREEK-STYLE

450 g (1 lb) young, unopened field mushrooms
150 ml (¼ pt) dry white wine
150 ml (¼ pt) water
60 ml (4 tbsp) olive oil (or vegetable oil, but the flavour is better with olive oil)
1 clove garlic, crushed
Juice of ½ lemon
6 black peppercorns, crushed
6 coriander seeds, crushed
1 bayleaf
1 sprig thyme (or 2.5 g/½ tsp dried)
2 or 3 parsley stalks (not leaves)
2.5 g (½ tsp) sugar
Salt
Parsley to garnish

Trim and wipe the mushrooms. Put all the ingredients except the mushrooms and garnish parsley into a pan, bring to the boil and simmer for 5 minutes. Put in the mushrooms, cover and simmer until just tender (3 or 4 minutes). Take out the mushrooms, draining off the liquid, and place in a dish. Boil remaining liquid quickly for a few minutes until reduced to about half, take out the herbs and pour over the mushrooms. Check seasoning and leave to cool in the refrigerator. Serve sprinkled with chopped parsley, with French bread to mop up the juices.
Serves 4 as a starter

STUFFED PEPPERS

Use just a few mushrooms if that is all you can find for this appetising lunch dish.

50 g (2 oz) field mushrooms (more if you have them)
15 ml (1 tbsp) vegetable oil
1 clove garlic, crushed
Black pepper
2 large red peppers
150 g (6 oz) cottage cheese
30 g (2 tbsp) diced cucumber
5 g (1 tsp) dried dill weed
2 stuffed olives

Clean and slice the mushrooms. Combine the oil, garlic and ground black pepper to taste and stir in a bowl with the mushrooms. Leave in the refrigerator for an hour or two, stirring occasionally, until the mushrooms are well marinated. Cut off the tops of the red peppers, and take out the seeds. Mix together the cheese, cucumber and dill weed, then stir in the mushrooms, drained of any surplus oil. Fill the peppers with the mixture and decorate with the olives, sliced. Serve with wholemeal bread and a green salad.
Serves 2

CRISPY RABBIT PIE

Hind legs and back joints of 2 young rabbits (wild if possible)
1 large onion
225 g (8 oz) field mushrooms
180 g (6 oz) fresh white breadcrumbs
600 ml (1 pt) milk
45 g (3 tbsp) parsley
1 egg
Salt and pepper
Butter or margarine

Place the rabbit pieces in a greased piedish. Finely chop the onion, peel and slice the mushrooms. Tuck the onion and mushrooms round the rabbit pieces. In a bowl mix the crumbs, milk, finely chopped parsley and lightly beaten egg and season generously. Spread this over the rabbit and dot surface with butter.

Cook in a low oven 150°C/300°F (Gas 2) for about 2 hours or until the rabbit feels tender when tested with a skewer and the topping is crisp and brown. (Cover with foil during cooking if the top becomes too brown too soon). Serve with new carrots and any green vegetable.
Serves 4

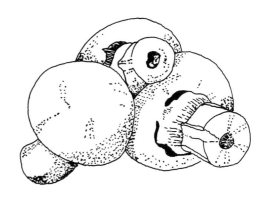

WIG OMELETTE
4 eggs
30 ml (2 tbsp) water
Salt and pepper
4 lawyer's wig mushrooms
50 g (2 oz) butter
30 g (2 tbsp) cooked peas

Beat the eggs and the water together and season with salt and pepper. Scrape off outer skin of the mushrooms, trim stalks and cut carefully into quarters lengthways.

Melt half the butter in a large frying or omelette pan, pour in the egg mixture and arrange the mushrooms radiating out from the middle like the spokes of a wheel. Dot the mushrooms with the remaining butter. Allow the omelette just to set over the heat, then put it under the grill and leave until the mushrooms are cooked and the omelette set and lightly browned (it will have risen a little). Sprinkle with hot cooked peas and cut in half to serve. It is good with salad and wholemeal bread and butter or any kind of potatoes. The mushrooms cook very quickly and in this simple dish retain their delicate flavour.
Serves 2

Shaggy ink caps are also good in scrambled egg. In this case, melt a little butter in a saucepan and simmer a very little chopped onion in it until the onion is transparent but not brown. Beat the eggs with salt and pepper and a little milk. Clean the mushrooms and chop into pieces. Cook for a minute in the butter, with the onion, then add the egg mixture and stir all together until creamy. Serve on hot buttered toast, garnished with watercress.

Puff ball

HOT PRAWN AND PUFFBALL 'SNACK'
25 g (1 oz) butter
100 g (4 oz) puffballs
100 g (4 oz) peeled prawns
1.25 g (¼ tsp) grated nutmeg
Tiny pinch hot chilli powder

Heat butter in a small pan, add the washed and sliced (or halved if small) puffballs, the prawns and spices. Toss until the prawns are heated through and the puffballs tender. Serve on hot buttered brown toast with slices of lemon and parsley to garnish.
Serves 2

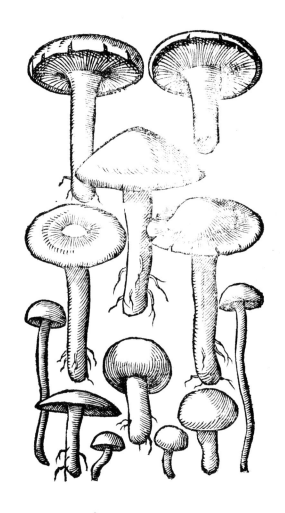

Field mushroom

PUFFERS WITH SORREL SAUCE
4–6 puffballs for each serving
For the batter
50 g (2 oz) plain flour
Pinch salt
Yolks of 2 eggs
30 ml (2 tbsp) double cream
30 ml (2 tbsp) water
White of 1 egg
Fat or oil for frying
Sorrel sauce (see page 99)

Clean the puffballs. Sift flour and salt into a basin, then add egg yolks, cream and water gradually to form a smooth batter. Leave in the refrigerator for at least 1 hour, then stir in the stiffly beaten egg white. Heat the fat until smoking. Dip the puffballs in the batter, fry in the hot fat until cooked through, drain on kitchen paper and keep hot. Serve with sorrel sauce (see page 99) as a starter or savoury.

Parasol mushrooms are VERY BIG and one is almost too much for one person to eat.

PORK WITH PARASOLS
50 g (2 oz) margarine or butter
900 g (2 lb) diced pork (or chicken if preferred)
1 clove garlic, crushed
Medium onion, finely sliced
15 g (1 tbsp) coriander seeds, crushed
Salt and pepper
225 g (8 oz) parasols, peeled and chopped
50 g (2 oz) walnuts, chopped
225 g (8 oz) courgettes, finely sliced
25 g (1½ tbsp) flour
Milk and water

Melt margarine in a pan and put in pork, garlic, onion, coriander seeds and seasoning. Fry gently until pork and onions are beginning to become tender. Add mushrooms, walnuts and courgettes and continue to cook until the meat and vegetables are tender. Stir in flour, cook a little, then mix in sufficient mixed milk and water to form a creamy sauce. Adjust seasoning and cook until sauce has thickened. Serve with brown rice and peas with lettuce (see page 72). Serves 4

SIMPLE PARASOL VEGETARIAN DISH
2 or more parasol mushrooms
450 g (1 lb) cold boiled potatoes
Any leftover cooked vegetables – runner beans, peas, cauliflower, etc
3 or 4 small tomatoes
Salt and pepper
Chopped herbs to taste (lovage, marjoram, etc.)
Butter or margarine

Peel and clean parasol mushrooms and chop up coarsely. Mix with the potatoes, diced, chopped-up vegetables, salt and pepper and herbs. Melt some butter or margarine in a pan and fry the mixture, adding a little more fat if necessary. When the mixture is hot, with crispy bits in it, it is ready as a tasty supper or lunch dish.
Serves 2–4 depending on appetite

STUFFED PARASOLS
4 parasol mushrooms
225 g (8 oz) boiled ham
25 g (1 oz) butter or margarine
25 g (1½ tbsp) flour
300 ml (½ pt) milk
30 g (2 tbsp) chopped parsley
7.5 ml (½ tbsp) lemon juice
Salt and pepper
Butter for cooking
Oatmeal

Peel the parasol mushrooms, detach and chop the stalks. Chop the boiled ham.

Melt the butter, stir in the flour and cook for a few minutes. Off the heat, stir in the milk and then cook until thick over a low heat, stirring. Stir in the parsley, lemon juice and salt and pepper, then the boiled ham and chopped mushroom stalks.

Melt a little butter in a large frying pan. Put in the mushrooms top side down and top each with the ham and sauce mixture. Sprinkle with oatmeal. Fry for a short time to cook the mushrooms underneath. Dot the tops with butter and put under the grill. Cook until heated through, then serve with green salad.
Serves 4

Coprinus comatus, shaggy ink cap *or* Lawyer's Wig

CREAMED PUFFBALLS FOR BREAKFAST

450 g (1 lb) small puffballs
150 ml ($\frac{1}{4}$ pt) milk
2 or 3 sprigs fresh thyme or 2.5 g ($\frac{1}{2}$ tsp) dried thyme
Salt and pepper
Yolks of 2 large eggs
30 ml (2 tbsp) double cream

Wash or wipe and slice the puffballs into 6-mm ($\frac{1}{4}$-in) slices and simmer in the milk with the thyme, salt and pepper until tender. Lightly mix together the egg yolks and cream with a fork. Off the heat, mix the egg and cream with the milk and puffballs. Stir gently over a low heat until the sauce thickens. Serve in individual small dishes with fingers of hot buttered toast.
Serves 4

LYCOPERDON CRAB SOUFFLES

2 small dressed crabs
5 ml (1 tsp) lemon juice
2 small slices of brown bread, made into crumbs
30 ml (2 tbsp) top of the milk or single cream
Black pepper to taste
2 large eggs
100 g (4 oz) puffballs, cleaned and finely chopped

Preheat the oven to 190°C/375°F (Gas 5). Scoop out the crabmeat and mix with the lemon juice, breadcrumbs, pepper and cream. Whisk eggs until well mixed and light. Fold eggs into crab-meat mixture, then fold in the puffballs. Put into 4 or 6 ramekins. Cook soufflés for 30–40 minutes until risen and browned, but not dry. Serve with cucumber and lemon garnish.
Serves 4–6

Galium aparine

GOOSEGRASS

Goosegrass, or cleavers, is every child's joke. Pull some out of the hedgerow and throw it at your friends – it sticks firmly to their backs and makes them look ridiculous as they walk along. As a blood purifier, it was used in Spring broths, as it is an early plant to make its appearance in hedgerows and along fields. In the past the seeds have been dried and ground to form a kind of coffee, and the young leaves can be used in salads. It is a minor food plant which repays experiment as it is green and prolific for a large part of the year.

POTATO SALAD WITH GOOSEGRASS
450 g (1 lb) new potatoes
60 ml (4 tbsp) mayonnaise
5 ml (1 tsp) lemon juice
30 g (2 tbsp) young goosegrass leaves and tips, finely chopped
Salt and pepper

Scrub the new potatoes without peeling them and cook until tender in boiling salted water. Drain and cut while still hot into cubes. While still warm, stir in the mayonnaise and lemon juice. Leave to cool, then stir in the goosegrass. Taste and correct seasoning if necessary. Serve at room temperature.
Serves 4

Other ideas:
Early in the year, when fresh salad greens are rare, the young shoots and leaves may be used as a salad ingredient with chickweed, dandelion leaves, finely chopped sprouts (surprisingly good, these) and a few chopped nuts – all with a good dressing, of course. Chopped up, you can add the tender shoots and leaves to soup, or mix with other wild greens as a vegetable accompaniment.

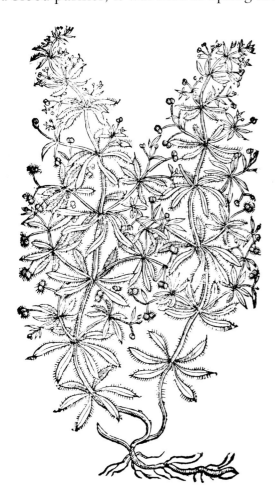

Goosegrass

Heracleum sphondylium

HOGWEED

The hogweed or cow parsnip grows prolifically in hedgerows throughout the summer months, bearing large umbels of white or pinkish flowers. Identify it carefully, as some other *umbelliferae* such as hemlock are very poisonous and should on no account be eaten.

The young stems are fleshy, full of flavour and good both on their own as well as cooked with other ingredients. I have to confess that I have not tried the following late 18th/early 19th century recipes, unadventurous as I might seem! 'The inhabitants of Kamtchatka, about the beginning of July, collect the foot-stalks of the radical leaves, and after peeling off the rind, which is very acrid, dry them separately in the sun, and then tying them in bundles, lay them up carefully in bags placed in the shade where they become covered with a yellow saccharine efflorescence, tasting like liquorice, which being shaken off, is eaten as a great delicacy. The Russians distil an ardent spirit from the stalks thus prepared, by first fermenting them in water with the great bilberries: and the spirit thus produced is said to be more agreeable to the taste than spirits made from corn.'

HOGWEED AS A VEGETABLE
Allow 8 or 9 tender stems, about 15-cm (6-in) long, for each serving. Tie with thread in bundles and drop into boiling salted water, cooking until tender (15–20 minutes). Drain and serve with a little butter as an accompaniment to meat.

WILD AND TAME 'VEGETABLE ZILDIC'
Mixture of vegetables – courgettes, Florence fennel, young carrots, cauliflower, French beans, peas, chopped hogweed stems, fat hen leaves, mallow leaves, plantain – whatever is available (to make about 900 g/2 lb in all).
For the sauce
50 g (2 oz) margarine
60 g (4 tbsp) flour
Salt and pepper
900 ml (1½ pt) mixed vegetable stock and milk
5 g (1 tsp) hot curry powder
1 clove garlic, crushed
Pinch each of ginger and nutmeg
50 g (2 oz) Cheddar cheese, grated
Sprinkling of Parmesan cheese

Lightly poach the prepared, sliced 'tame' vegetables in boiling salted water. Drain, reserving the vegetable stock. Wash and chop the 'wild' vegetables into small pieces. Put all the vegetables into a casserole.

Melt the margarine in a saucepan, add the flour and stir until absorbed. Remove from the heat and gradually add the stock and milk mixture, stirring all the time. Season lightly. When cooked, set aside half the white sauce. To one half add the curry powder, garlic, ginger and nutmeg and stir into the vegetables in the casserole. To the other half add the grated cheese, mixing well, and pour over the top of the dish. Sprinkle with Parmesan cheese.

Bake for about half-an-hour at 190°C/375°F (Gas 5) until the vegetables are tender and the top browned. Serve with potatoes or rice.
Serves 4

Heracleum sphondylium

HOPS

Before my interest in wild plant cookery arose, I used to think of hops as plants grown in Kent and used in brewing. However, I discovered that the young shoots of hop plants are excellent in any recipes using asparagus, and plainly boiled and served with butter, they are just as delicious – and free! The Romans knew this use too – it was described by the writer Pliny nearly 2,000 years ago – and as recently as a hundred years ago, hop tops were picked and sold in bundles as a vegetable. Now you can find the plants twining up in many a hedgerow and gather your own.

Later, when the pale green flowers are out, forming a beautiful contrast with the dark green, strawberry-like leaves, you might like to try them in a simple beer recipe. Hops were not used in brewing until comparatively late in the 14th century. Before that, other flavourings were used in fermented beverages. As hop flowers have sedative properties, they are often put into small pillows and sold as sleep-inducers. Make your own, or look out for them in herbal shops.

It is interesting to note that, even in the early 19th century, doctors were complaining about 'food additives' which were harmful to their patients. Here is one concerning beer, the British national drink, which forms an interesting social comment. 'That most abominable of all abominations tobacco is notoriously used as a substitute for the hop and green vitriol with other poisons too numerous to name are added (by the brewers) to mature the deleterious mixture. Hence it is that the poor mechanic is drawn into habitual inebriation. He cannot slake his thirst without causing it to return with greater force at very short intervals. Unconscious of the cause, he repeats the draught and the consequences are disease and premature and even sudden death.

When will the strong arm of power put a stop to these iniquities? When will our rulers extend it, to protect the health, morals and happiness of the community and arrest the deadly ravages of those unprincipled villains who wallow in ill-gotten wealth for a few years and then bequeath immense revenues for their descendants to scatter to the winds?'

Hops

62

Humulus lupulus

SPLIT PEA SOUP
225 g (8 oz) split peas
3 litres (5¼ pt) water
Small knuckle of bacon
1 medium onion
1 large potato
Sprig lovage
2.5 g (½ tsp) celery seeds
Bunch hop shoots

Soak the peas in the water overnight, and in a separate bowl soak the knuckle of bacon. Add the drained knuckle to the pan with the peas and water, together with the onion, peeled and finely sliced and the potato peeled and cubed, the lovage and the celery seeds. Simmer, stirring from time to time, until the peas are mushy, remove bacon knuckle and lovage and blend or sieve the soup. Lightly poach the chopped hop tops, shred up the meat from the knuckle. Return the soup to the pan, add the meat and hop shoots and reheat. Taste and correct seasoning before serving. This is a satisfying soup served with chunks of wholemeal bread and butter. Serves 6–8

SIMPLEST OF BEERS
75 g (3 oz) hop flowers
18 litres (4 gallons) water
625 g (1¼ lb) brown sugar
30 ml (2 tbsp) fresh yeast (or 1 packet dried brewers' yeast)

Boil the hops in the water for 60 to 90 minutes. Remove from heat and stir in the sugar until it dissolves. Strain into a plastic bucket with a lid. When the mixture is lukewarm, add the yeast, cover and leave in a warm place to work for two days. Skim well, strain through a muslin or cheesecloth into bottles. Cork and leave in a cool place for a few days before drinking.

HOP AND SHERRY TONIC
Fill a wide-necked jar with hop flowers, then fill to the top with a medium-sweet sherry. Allow to infuse for 3 weeks, then strain into clean, dry bottles and use.

HUMULUS QUICHE
150 g (6 oz) short-crust pastry (bought or made using 100 g (4 oz) flour, 50 g (2 oz) fat, pinch salt and water to mix)
1 medium onion, chopped
40 g (1½ oz) butter or margarine
300 ml (½ pt) milk
Small bay leaf
25 g (1 oz) flour
1 egg yolk
30 ml (2 tbsp) double cream
150 g (6 oz) young hop shoots chopped and lightly poached in boiling salted water
Salt and pepper
Sprinkling of nutmeg

Roll out the pastry thinly and line an 18–20 cm (7–8 in) flan dish. Prick the bottom with a fork and leave in the refrigerator. If there are any scraps of pastry left over, keep them to use as a decoration on top of the quiche.

Melt the butter and cook the onion until soft but not brown. While it is cooking, warm milk with bayleaf and leave to infuse for a few minutes. Stir the flour into the butter and onion mixture and stir in the strained milk gradually to make a smooth sauce. Return to heat and stir until the sauce comes to boiling point. Remove from heat. Mix together the egg yolk and cream and stir into the sauce. Add the hop shoots and seasoning. Pour into the prepared pastry case and decorate the top with a lattice of pastry strips or shapes. Bake at 220°C/425°F (Gas 7) for half-an-hour or until the pastry is lightly browned. Can be eaten hot or cold. Serves 4

HOP TOP BUTTER
100 g (4 oz) softened butter
100 g (4 oz) hop shoots

Cook the hop shoots in a tiny amount of boiling water until pulpy, then rub through a sieve. The resulting pulp should be very stiff. Work well into the butter. Add salt and pepper to taste. Form butter into a cylinder, wrap in foil and store in the freezer or refrigerator. Cut off slices to top hot grilled meat or fish as required. (Will keep for several days in refrigerator or weeks in freezer.)

WHITE AND RED DEAD NETTLE

Rather more exotic names for the dead nettles are White and Purple Archangel. They are both prolific growers on waste land and in hedgerows – Culpeper remarks that 'they grow almost everywhere, unless it be in the middle of the street' – and can be eaten as a vegetable alone or cooked in recipes. Bees love them and in some countries the white variety is known as 'Bee-nettle'. Pick the leaves, or flower heads when young. The white dead nettle has a stronger smell, but this fades with cooking. You will need a large quantity of the plants as they boil down considerably.

ARCHANGEL SOUFFLÉ
450 g (1 lb) potatoes (weighed after peeling)
Small onion
50 g (2 oz) red or white young dead nettle tips and flowers (if in bloom)
Salt and pepper
45 ml (3 tbsp) milk
2 eggs, separated
Butter

Chop up potatoes and onion and cook together in boiling salted water until soft. Drain. Cook nettles in a little boiling salt water until cooked and drain very thoroughly, pressing out all the water with the back of a spoon. Blend or sieve the vegetables together, season and beat in the milk and egg yolks. Grease an 850 ml (1½ pt) soufflé dish with butter. Beat the egg whites very stiffly and fold into the potato and nettle mixture. Put in a preheated oven at 200°C/400°F (Gas 6) for 30–35 minutes until risen and brown. This soufflé has the great advantage of not 'deflating' easily and is delicious as a potato accompaniment to cold meat as well as a dish in its own right.
Serves 4

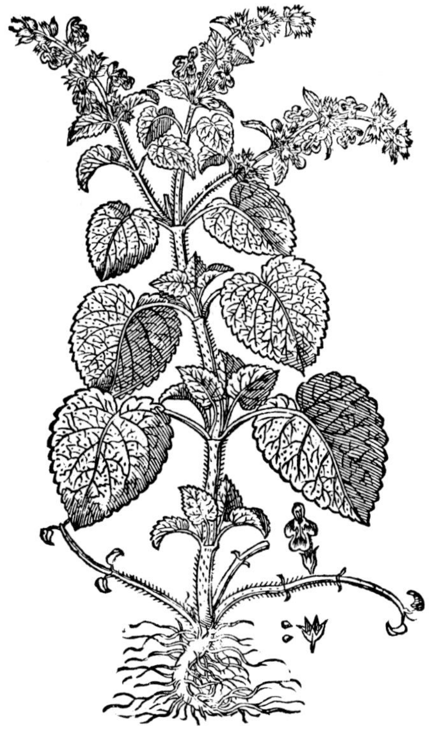

Hedge nettle

65

Above: *Lamium rubrum*, red dead nettle
Above left: *Lamium album*, white dead nettle

LAMIUM PIE

450 g (1 lb) red dead nettle tops and flowers
225 g (8 oz) puff pastry, thawed
150 g (6 oz) cottage cheese
25 ml (1½ tbsp) vegetable oil
1 egg, beaten
Ground black pepper
Beaten egg for glazing

Wash and dry the nettle tops and chop coarsely. Roll out the pastry as thinly as possible and line a shallow tin about 25 cm (10 in) by 15 cm (6 in). Put the remaining pastry and the lined tin to cool in the refrigerator. Mix the nettles with the cheese, oil, egg and pepper and put in the lined tin. Damp the pastry edges, roll out the remaining pastry and cover, pressing the edges well together. Brush the top with beaten egg. Heat the oven to 200°C/400°F (Gas 6) and put in the pie. Bake for 40–45 minutes until the pastry is brown. Serve hot with potatoes and/or green vegetable.
Serves 6

DEAD NETTLE TUMBLE

450 g (1 lb) young red or white dead nettle tops
6 eggs
30 ml (2 tbsp) milk
Seasoning
40 g (1½ oz) butter

Cook the dead nettle tops until tender in a little boiling salted water. Press to drain thoroughly, chop up finely. Beat the eggs with the milk and seasoning. Melt the butter in a saucepan, add the eggs and nettle tops and cook until creamy. Serve on hot buttered toast, sprinkled with a little nutmeg if liked, as a light supper dish.
Serves 4

Lamium album / Lamium purpureum

CRAB APPLE

The true crab apple tree, found in hedgerows and open places, is small and spiny and the apples round and yellow, or sometimes red. It is the ancestor of all our cultivated apples and has been used since ancient times. Consequently, there are many superstitions clinging to the fruit, its seeds and the trees on which it grows. You will find many varieties of crab apple descended from cultivated apples which have seeded and reverted to a wild form, or crossed with true crab apples to produce yet another variation, as shown here.

APPLE BUTTER
Crab apples
Dry cider
Sugar
Lemon juice and grated rind

Wash the crab apples and cut in half, without peeling. Put in a pan and cover with cider. Cook until pulpy, then press through a sieve. To every 600 ml (1 pt) pulp add 325 g ($\frac{3}{4}$ lb) sugar. Put back in the pan with lemon juice and grated rind and simmer for about an hour, stirring. Pour into heated jars and seal. Use fairly soon – this will not keep for too long or freeze in plastic containers.

POTATO CAKE WITH CRAB APPLE
BUTTER
450 g (1 lb) cooked potatoes
25 g (1 oz) butter
5 g (1 tsp) brown sugar
1.25 g ($\frac{1}{4}$ tsp) cinnamon
100 g (4 oz) flour
Crab apple butter (see above)

Mash the hot potatoes with the butter, sugar and cinnamon and blend in the flour to form a 'pastry' which can be rolled out. Form into two rounds about 13 mm ($\frac{1}{2}$-in) deep, one slightly larger in diameter than the other. Cover the smaller round thickly with crabapple butter, moisten the edge, cover with the other round and press both rounds together, fluting with the back of a spoon or with a fork. With a knife, mark cuts across the top and bake at 230°C/450°F (Gas 8) for about 30 minutes until the top is browned and the pastry cooked through. Carefully remove the top 'crust' and dot the apple butter with extra dairy butter and brown sugar.

WASSAIL
This potent brew might be one to try for a party. If you want to use 'roasted crabs' in true Shakespearean form in a Christmas drink you will have to freeze some.

600 ml (1 pt) strong ale
450 g (1 lb) brown sugar
5 g (1 tsp) grated nutmeg
Small piece preserved stem ginger or fresh ginger root, chopped
150 ml ($\frac{1}{4}$ pt) medium sherry
3 litres ($5\frac{1}{4}$ pt) bitter beer
Yeast
Apples

Heat the strong ale and dissolve the sugar in it. Take off the heat and add the nutmeg, ginger and sherry, stirring well. Mix in a covered container with the bitter beer and sprinkle a little dried yeast on top (or float a piece of toast with a spreading of fresh yeast). Leave in a warm, but not hot, place for 3 or 4 hours, then strain into screw-top bottles and keep for a few days, when it should be 'lively'. Pour into a large bowl and float on the top some crabapples which have been roasted to bursting point in a hot oven.

Malus sylvestris

Malva sylvestris

MALLOW

The common mallow, with its dark leaves and handsome purple flowers, blooms in the hedgerows for many weeks. The young leaves may be cooked as a vegetable (again, it was eaten by the Romans). Its main interest in cookery is that the leaves exude a gelatinous substance very similar to that given out by a plant which grows in Middle Eastern countries. This is used to make a well-known soup called Melokhia, and you can make your own version with our common mallow. When I chopped up the leaves for the recipe given below, I could feel the gelatinous juice slimy on my fingers. This may not sound very pleasant, but in fact the soup is delicious, with a hot, invigorating flavour. It seems not to kill the appetite for the next course, but stimulates the digestive juices to even greater efforts.

MALLOW SOUP
225 g (8 oz) young mallow leaves
1 litre (1¾ pt) strong chicken stock (or use 2 chicken stock cubes and 600 ml water)
2 large cloves garlic
10 g (2 tsp) coriander seeds
5 g (1 tsp) salt (preferably sea salt)
30 ml (2 tbsp) vegetable oil

Finely chop the cleaned mallow leaves. Heat the stock to boiling point, add the leaves and cook for at least 20 minutes, until the leaves are tender. Pound the garlic, coriander seeds and salt together. Heat the oil and cook the seasonings in it for a minute or two, being careful they do not burn. Stir the seasonings into the soup and cook for a few minutes, stirring. Serve with chunks of white bread and unsalted butter. Slivers of cooked poultry or meat may be added for a more substantial soup.
Serves 4

FISH SOUP
450 g (1 lb) prawns in the shell
450 g (1 lb) white fish
1 litre (1¾ pt) water
Pepper
Bouquet of mixed herbs – bayleaf, thyme, fennel, parsley
Small onion, quartered
225 g (8 oz) tomatoes
50 g (2 oz) young mallow leaves
150 ml (¼ pt) dry white wine
30 ml (2 tbsp) tomato purée
15 ml (1 tbsp) mushroom ketchup or Worcestershire sauce
Chopped parsley to garnish

Shell the prawns, skin the fish. Put the shells and trimmings in the water with the pepper, herbs and onion. Bring to the boil and simmer for about 30 minutes. Cut the fish into small strips and skin and slice the tomatoes. Wash and chop the mallow leaves. Strain the fish stock into a clean pan, add the mallow leaves, and simmer for about 20 minutes. Add the prawns and fish, tomatoes, wine, tomato purée and ketchup, reheat and simmer for a further 5 minutes or until the fish is cooked. Serve sprinkled with plenty of parsley and with French bread. Serves 4

Malva sylvestris

Mentha arvensis/Mentha aquatica

MINT

Mint is an ancient herb, reputed to have been named after Minthe, a nymph loved by Pluto whose jealous wife turned her into a plant. It is also mentioned in the Bible as one of the tithes paid to the Romans. It used to be a favourite strewing herb and was also used to give a fresh perfume to bath water.

There are so many varieties of mint growing wild that I have chosen just two. Mint can be used for such a wide variety of recipes that it is difficult to know where to begin. Try out several wild varieties and see which subtle variation in flavour you prefer. Incidentally, some expert cooks say you should never make a mint sauce for lamb as so many of us do, using vinegar and sugar, but simply put a mint bunch under the lamb when it is roasting. This gives it a delicate flavour and a minty taste to the gravy juices. Medicinally, mint has always been used as an aid to digestion and for stomach troubles, though tradition has it that if you give it to a wounded man, he will not recover!

CUCUMBER AND WATER MINT SOUP
2 medium-sized cucumbers or 1 large one
1 small onion
2 cloves garlic
5 large sprigs water mint
Salt and pepper
420 g (15 oz) carton natural yoghurt (or 450 g/ 1 lb)
300 ml ($\frac{1}{2}$ pt) cold chicken stock and milk, mixed
Double cream
Mint leaves to garnish

Wipe but do not peel the cucumbers. Grate them. Peel and grate the onion and press the garlic to extract the juice. Mix cucumber, onion and garlic together. Strip the washed mint leaves from the stem and chop them finely. Combine the cucumber mixture and mint with the yoghurt and stock. Chill in the refrigerator for at least an hour and serve in chilled bowls each with a swirl of cream and a mint leaf to garnish.
Serves 4

PEAS AND LETTUCE WITH WILD MINT
15 g ($\frac{1}{2}$ oz) butter
4 or 5 large outer leaves of lettuce (preferably a crisp one) washed but not dried
1 small onion, finely chopped
450 g (1 lb) fresh or frozen peas
5 g (1 tsp) sugar
3 or 4 sprigs of corn mint, chopped
Salt and pepper

Grease the bottom of a pan with the butter. Shred the lettuce finely. Put some of the lettuce in the bottom of the pan, sprinkle with a little of the onion, then put in some peas, seasoning, a few grains of sugar and some chopped mint. Continue to fill the pan with the ingredients until all are used up. Do not add water.

Cover and put on a low heat. Shake the pan from time to time to prevent sticking. The vegetable is ready when the peas are cooked and the lettuce has simmered down into a soft purée with the mint and onion. Delicious with lamb chops. Serves 4

Mentha arvensis / Mentha aquatica

LIVER WITH WATER MINT

450 g (1 lb) calves' liver
150 ml (¼ pt) beef stock
1 medium onion
1 clove garlic
15 g (1 tbsp) water mint, finely chopped
75 ml (⅛ pt) red wine vinegar

Slice the liver thinly, seal in the hot stock for a minute or two until brown. Finely chop the onion and crush the garlic, remove liver from the stock and put in the onion and garlic, simmering until soft. Add the vinegar and mint, put the meat back in the pan, adding a little more stock if necessary, season to taste and cover. Simmer for 8–10 minutes until the liver is tender. Serve with rice and peas.
Serves 4

MINT AND APPLE SORBET

450 g (1 lb) well-flavoured eating apples
300 ml (½ pt) water
100 g (4 oz) sugar
150 ml (¼ pt) medium sweet white wine
30 g (2 tbsp) corn mint leaves, finely chopped
Whites of 2 eggs

Wash and chop up the apples (including skin and core) put in a pan with the water and sugar and simmer until soft and pulpy. Cool and press through a sieve. When cold, mix in the wine and mint, place in a container and freeze until slushy.

Whisk the egg whites until stiff and stir into the purée. Freeze again until solid. Serve decorated with slices of fresh apple and crystallised mint leaves (see Primrose recipe, page 78).
Serves 4–6

Spearmint

Red garden mint

CAPTAIN MARRYAT'S MINT JULEP

Make each person's drink as follows: Into a tumbler put about a dozen tender mint leaves (bruised) – any type of wild mint will do. Upon them put a spoonful of white sugar and equal portions of peach and ordinary brandy to fill the tumbler up to about one third. Fill up with crushed ice – and for a really epicurean flavour rub around the lip of the tumbler with a piece of fresh pineapple.

For a more ordinary julep, try the following (also an American recipe). Into a tumbler put a lump of sugar and a few drips of water to dissolve it. Pour in 1 wineglassful (or double measure) of whisky (or gin or brandy if you prefer), add 1 or 2 sprigs of mint, bruised, and a little crushed ice. Decorate the top with a small slice of orange and one of pineapple. Serve at once.

DRINKING YOGHURT

If you can buy liquid drinking yoghurt, you can liven it up for summer drinking by adding a few teaspoons of chopped wild mint, stirring and chilling before use.

WATER-MINTY CIDER

7 or 8 sprigs water (or other) mint
300 ml ($\frac{1}{2}$ pt) each of orange and apple juice
Juice of 2 lemons
45 g (3 tbsp) sugar
600 ml (1 pt) sweet cider

Wash and bruise the mint. Mix in a bowl with all the other ingredients except the cider. Stand the mixture to infuse for an hour, then chill. Strain, add cider and mix well just before serving. Pour over ice in individual glasses and decorate with extra mint sprigs.

WATER MINT CREAM ICE

1 handful of water mint
300 ml ($\frac{1}{2}$ pt) milk
Yolks of 6 eggs
75 g (3 oz) sugar
300 ml ($\frac{1}{2}$ pt) double cream
Green food colouring
50 g (2 oz) chocolate chips

Wash and chop the mint coarsely and put with the milk in a pan. Bring to the boil, cover and leave to infuse for 10 minutes off heat. Strain the milk, throwing the mint away.

Beat together the egg yolks and sugar, mix with the milk and stir over a low heat (preferably in a double boiler or basin in a pan of hot water) until thick. Remove from heat and continue to stir for a minute or two, then set aside to cool.

Whip the cream until thick and fold into the cold mint custard. Colour pale green with food colouring and add the chocolate chips. Put in freezing trays and place in the freezer, stirring once or twice during freezing to break up the ice crystals. Makes 4–6 portions

ECCLES CAKES WITH CORN MINT

225 g (8 oz) flour
2.5 g ($\frac{1}{2}$ tsp) salt
50 g (2 oz) lard
50 g (2 oz) melted butter or margarine
100 g (4 oz) brown sugar
125 g (5 oz) currants
Grated rind of 1 small lemon
30 g (2 tbsp) corn mint leaves, finely chopped

Preheat oven to 220°C/450°F (Gas 8). Sift flour and salt together and rub in the lard and butter until the mixture resembles breadcrumbs. Lightly mix in enough cold water to form a stiff dough. Roll out on a floured board to 5 mm ($\frac{1}{8}$ in) thick.

Using a 10-cm (4-in) cutter cut the pastry into rounds. Mix together the rest of the ingredients. Put 30 or 45 g (2 or 3 tsp) on each pastry round. Brush edges with water and press together to enclose the filling. Turn each cake over and flatten with a rolling pin. Cut 2 slits in the top of each, sprinkle with caster sugar and bake for 15–20 minutes until pale brown. Makes 16–18

Plantago lanceolata, p. major

PLANTAIN

Once in seven years the
plantain turns into a cuckoo.
(Old Devonshire saying)

The ribwort plantain is much liked by grazing animals and the seeds of all varieties appreciated by birds.

The recumbent great plantain appears to flourish the more it is trodden on and it used to be known as 'Englishman's foot' by the North American Indians as it seemed to spring up wherever white men lived and worked.

Plantain is said to be a cure for rattle-snake bite and in times long ago the Assembly of South Carolina, USA, gave a considerable reward to a negro, Caesar by name, who invented a remedy for snakebites using plantain among other ingredients.

Plantain is one of the plants mentioned in the Saxon 'nine herbs charm', each herb being used for healing a different type of illness. The herbalist would chant the correct section of verse as he administered the remedy.

And thou, Plantain, Mother of herbs
Open from the East, mighty within,
Over thee chariots creaked, over thee queens
   rode,
Over thee brides made outcry, over thee
   bulls gnashed their teeth
All these thou didst withstand and resist;
So mayest thou withstand poison and
   infection,
And the foe who fares through the land.

(Quoted from *Mastering Herbalism*, Paul Huson)

This is a plant which should be picked very young, and, if cooked, it should be done thoroughly as it tends to be tough. The leaves have a nutty flavour and a small quantity of delicate central leaves may be used, finely chopped in a mixed or rice salad.

CHICKEN AND PLANTAIN CREAM

225 g (8 oz) young plantain leaves
50 g (2 oz) butter
700 g (1½ lb) raw chicken flesh, diced in small
   pieces
50 g (2 oz) walnuts
Salt and ground black pepper
300 ml (½ pt) double cream

Wash the plantain leaves, having discarded any tough stems, put in boiling salted water and cook until tender. Drain well and chop. Melt the butter in a frying pan and toss the chicken in it until it begins to colour. Roughly chop the walnuts and add them with the plantain leaves to the pan and cook together for a further 5 to 8 minutes. Season, then add the double cream, scraping up and amalgamating it with the buttery juices. Stir for 5 minutes or so until the cream thickens. Serve with plain boiled potatoes or rice and a green vegetable.
Serves 4

PLANTAIN WITH BAKED EGGS

For each serving allow 50 g (2 oz) plantain leaves, 15 ml (1 tbsp) double cream, a knob of butter, salt, pepper, a little nutmeg and an egg. Boil the chopped plantain leaves until tender, drain well and mix with a very little butter, half the cream, salt and pepper. Put in the bottom of a lightly-buttered ramekin. Break an egg on top of the plantain, spoon over the rest of the cream and sprinkle with nutmeg. Bake in a moderate oven until the eggs are set to your liking. Serve with fingers of hot brown toast.

Plantago lanceolata, plantago major

Primula vulgaris

PRIMROSE

When great clumps of primroses are in flower in the hedgerows, looking like heaps of clotted cream, one begins to feel that warm weather is really on the way. These days it is the cowslip (*Primula veris*), once so plentiful and widely used for country wines and creams, which is becoming rare, and should not be picked. Primroses were used in many of the same recipes, but again, please be sparing and use them rather as a novelty and decoration than in quantity.

Culpeper writes that the best way to use primroses is to bruise the roots and express the juice 'which being snuffed up the nose occasions violent sneezing and brings away a great deal of water, but without being productive of any bad effect'.

If you keep hens, remember the old country superstition and do not bring less than 13 primroses into the house or they will never hatch out good broods.

TO CANDY PRIMROSES
Pick the flowers when they are just open, leaving a little of the stem on so that they can be handled more easily. You will need greaseproof paper or foil, very lightly beaten egg white, a small paintbrush, caster sugar and a very fine sieve (optional).

Pick up each flower by the stem and paint all over with egg white, using the paintbrush. Dust with the sugar, either sprinkling it on by hand or through the sieve. Cut off the stem and place flower on the paper or foil and leave to harden in the airing cupboard or similar warm dry place (but not in the sun). When dry, store in airtight jars. Violets, rose petals, mint leaves and borage flowers may be treated in the same way, to give just a few examples.

PRIMROSE SYRUP
(Only make if there are plenty of primroses around)

225 g (8 oz) primrose flowers
400 ml ($\frac{2}{3}$ pt) water
225 g (8 oz) sugar

Simmer the flowers, water and sugar together until a thick syrup is formed. Strain, bottle and use with plain ice cream or mixed with soda and ice for a refreshing drink.

PRIMROSES IN SALADS
Add a few petals and chopped young leaves to spring salads for a novel taste and pretty decoration.

PRIMROSE TEA
To each cup of petals add 7 cups of boiling water and leave to infuse. Strain and serve sweetened with a little honey.

Primula vulgaris

WILD CHERRY

Keep your mouth open for a ripe cherry.
(Welsh saying)

Wild cherries are smaller and more sour than the cultivated variety, and can never be eaten uncooked with any pleasure. However the tree's white delicate blossom is beautiful in spring and the fruit is very good in cooking as it has a fine flavour. You have to pick the cherries fairly unripe as when they begin to turn colour the blackbirds are very partial to them. The few cherries that survive on the tree I know turn a very dark red when ripe, but their bitterness is unchanged. A nice old name for the wild cherry is 'Merries', presumably a corruption of the French 'cerise'.

According to Lucullus, the cherry was known in Asia in the Roman year 680, so it is a tree of great antiquity.

SOUR CHERRY SOUP
450 g (1 lb) wild cherries (stoned)
3 or 4 rusks
1.5 litres (3 pt) water
Small piece cinnamon stick
Lemon rind
25 g (1 oz) butter
15 g ($\frac{1}{2}$ oz) flour
150 ml ($\frac{1}{4}$ pt) white wine
100 g (4 oz) sugar
Pinch salt

Put the stoned cherries in a pan. Break the cherry stones, remove the kernels and add to the cherries. Put in the water and rusks, broken up, the cinnamon and grated rind of half a lemon. Simmer for 20 minutes, then rub through a sieve. Melt the butter, add the flour and stir until they are amalgamated. Stir in the wine, then add the cherry pulp, sugar and salt. Reheat until the soup thickens and serve hot or cold.
Serves 6

WILD CHERRY SYRUP
900 g (2 lb) ripe wild cherries
225 g (8 oz) sugar

Stone the cherries and press the fruit with a wooden spoon. Add the sugar and 30–60 ml (2–4 tbsp) water and bring to the boil. Skim. When cool, press through a sieve and bottle. Use on vanilla icecream or, diluted with soda and with ice added, as a refreshing drink.

FRENCH CHERRY FLAN
450 g (1 lb) cherries, stoned
225 g (8 oz) sugar
Sprig eau-de-cologne mint
15-cm (6-in) cooked sweet pastry flan case
Peel from two or three cooking apples
300 ml ($\frac{1}{2}$ pt) whipping cream

Stew together the cherries, sugar and mint until the cherries are tender. Drain cherries, reserving juice, and remove the mint. Put the drained cherries in the flan case.

Stew the apple peel in the cherry syrup until reduced to about half. Strain and leave the juice in a bowl in the refrigerator until it begins to set. Pour over the cherries in the flan case and leave until cold and firm. Whip the cream and pipe or spoon on the flan to decorate. Serves 4

Prunus avium

CHERRY BRANDY
450 g (1 lb) cherries (not over-ripe)
75 g (3 oz) caster sugar
Brandy to cover

Cut off the cherry stalks, leaving them about ½-in in length. Wipe the cherries with a cloth and put them into a wide-necked bottle, filling it a little more than half full, and layering the cherries with the sugar. Fill up with brandy, seal closely and leave for at least two months before straining off and using.

CHERRY PUDDING
450 g (1 lb) ripe wild cherries
45 g (3 tbsp) moist brown sugar
Small piece cinnamon stick
50 g (2 oz) flour
50 g (2 oz) caster sugar
4 eggs
75 ml (⅛ pt) single cream
30 ml (2 tbsp) milk
Grated rind of ½ lemon
Salt

Stone the cherries and put them with the cinnamon, brown sugar and 30 ml (2 tbsp) water in a jar. Place in a saucepan of boiling water, cook until tender and allow to cool. Heat the cream, add the flour, blended smoothly with the milk, cook very briefly, add the caster sugar and a pinch of salt. Allow to cool a little, then beat in the yolks of the eggs, the lemon rind and lastly the stiffly whipped egg whites. In a buttered mould place a layer of cherries, then a layer of the mixture and repeat until full. Cover with a buttered paper and bake at 190°C/375°F (Gas 5) for 40–60 minutes. Serve with custard or cream.
4–6 portions

CHERRY JAM
450 g (1 lb) ripe cherries
450 g (1 lb) granulated sugar
150 ml (¼ pt) water

Stone the cherries and crack the stones to remove the kernels. Put the water and sugar in a pan and boil to form a syrup. Add the cherries and kernels and simmer until the cherries are tender and the juice 'jells' when a little is poured on a cold plate. Pour into sterile jars and cover in the usual way.

WILD CHERRY COMPÔTE
450 g (1 lb) cherries, stoned
225 g (8 oz) sugar
2 or 3 drops almond essence
15 ml (1 tbsp) water

Simmer all together until the cherries are tender. Serve hot or cold with a plain chocolate icecream on top of each serving.
Serves 4

CHERRY-FLAVOURED BEER
450 g (1 lb) wild cherries
450 g (1 lb) granulated sugar
1.7 litres (3 pt) strong ale
Sachet ale yeast

Wash the cherries and prick them all over with a skewer. Put in a large wide-necked container. Dissolve the sugar in the ale and pour it over the cherries. Add the yeast, cover and leave to ferment in a warm place. When fermentation has finished, move the container to a cooler place to let the sediment settle. Strain and bottle in sterilised bottles and store in a cool, dark place for three months before drinking.

CHERRY BOUNCE
Cherries
To each 600 ml (1 pt) of juice allow the following:
225 g (8 oz) sugar
Pinch each of ground mace and ground allspice
300 ml (½ pt) brandy
300 ml (½ pt) rum

To prepare the cherries, remove the stones and place the fruit in a large jar. Stand the jar in a saucepan of boiling water, cook gently until all the juice is extracted, strain it into a preserving or other large pan and measure. Add the sugar, mace and allspice and simmer and skim until the scum ceases to rise. When cold, add the spirits and bottle for use.

BULLACE

This is the ancestor of the garden plum, and its sub-species name appears in an old botanical reference book I possess, which remarks that the acid fruit is 'not unpleasant, especially after it is mellowed by frost'. Pliny stated that the trees came from Syria into Greece and thence to Italy – and our friends the Romans, in whose debt we must always be for all the plants they carried with them, probably brought cuttings to Britain, which have since reverted to the wild form. The recipe given below was originally for sloe gin – but it can be used with bullaces for novelty.

BULLACE GIN
Bullaces
Gin
Sugar

Prick the bullaces all over with a fine skewer or darning needle and half fill a wide-necked bottle with them. Fill up with gin, cork or put the lid on the bottle and leave for ten days. Strain off the liquid, replenish the jar with fresh bullaces, pour back the gin, topping up with fresh spirit if necessary. Leave for another ten days, strain again and add 100 g (4 oz) sugar to each 600 ml (1 pt) of gin. Bottle for use. (Shake or turn the bottles occasionally to make sure all the sugar is melted).

Do not waste the gin-soaked bullaces. All fruit used in this way for fruit liqueurs or drinks may be cooked afterwards in the usual way for making jam or preserves. It has a 'gourmet' taste and certainly livens up the breakfast toast. Or try it on scones, topped with cream, for an English tea.

PICKLED BULLACES
Bullaces
Pickling vinegar

Pick the bullaces while still hard, and simmer for a few minutes in boiling water. Drain and pack into jars. Make up a pickling vinegar, using to each pint of malt vinegar, a piece of fresh root ginger, chopped, clove of sliced garlic, mixed pickling spice and 10 g (2 tsp) brown sugar. Simmer all together, and pour hot over the bullaces. Seal in the usual way. Leave for a month before eating.

BULLACE BUTTER
900 g (2 lb) ripe bullaces
Sugar

Cook the bullaces until soft, adding a little water if necessary to stop burning. When cooked, rub through a sieve to extract the stones. Return to the pan and continue cooking until thick and quite dry. To each 450 g (1 lb) purée add 350 g ($\frac{3}{4}$ lb) sugar and stir off the heat until dissolved. Then continue to cook until very thick (so thick that the stirring spoon leaves a mark when run across the surface). Put into jars and press cling film on the surface. When cool seal top in usual way.

Prunus spinosa

SLOE

When the sloe tree is as white as a sheet,
sow your barley whether it be dry or wet.
(Old Country saying)

The other name for the sloe is 'blackthorn', and it grows in many hedgerows, a tough, black, spiny bush covered with a cloud of white blossoms early in the year, before its leaves appear. If you have ever tried to gather the tempting purple clusters of sloes you will know how painful a wound from the spines or thorns can be, and it is no wonder that formerly the wood was used as the teeth of rakes. Many uses for the sloe have been quoted. Its leaves were once dried and used as a substitute for tea, but they were often coloured or treated with a poisonous substance to make them look like genuine Indian tea until 'these practices were discovered and justly punished'. Letters marked upon linen or woollen cloth with the juice of this fruit will 'not wash out' says the same 19th-century authority, and 'bruised and put into wine it communicates a beautiful red colour and there is, in fact, too much reason to presume that this juice enters largely into the British manufacture of Port wine.'

Sloe gin acquired its name of 'Mother's Ruin' in past centuries, as the sloes were mixed with pennyroyal mint and valerian and used as an abortifacient – and a bitter drink it must have been.

Always pick your sloes after they have been frosted, as they are then mellowed. Use either the recipe method given for bullaces to make sloe gin, or the other method below. I think the fruit needs the addition of apples if used for preserves or pies.

SLOE AND APPLE JELLY CREAMS
450 g (1 lb) sloes
900 g (2 lb) cooking apples
Sugar
600 ml (1 pt) whipped cream

Put the sloes in a pan and cover with water. Bring to the boil and simmer until soft. Wash and roughly chop the apples (no need to peel). Put in a pan with one or two tablespoons of water and simmer until pulpy. Drain the sloes and keep the juice. Press the apple through a sieve. Mix together the sloe juice and pulped apple and to each 450 g (1 lb) add 225 g (8 oz) light brown sugar. Return to the pan and simmer together until a little placed on a cool saucer wrinkles when pushed with the finger. Leave to go cold and set slightly, then layer into goblets with whipped cream. Leave to set in the refrigerator before serving, sprinkled with a little grated chocolate if liked.
Serves 6

SLOE GIN
450 g (1 lb) sloes
150 g (6 oz) sugar
Few drops almond essence or 25 g (1 oz) flaked almonds
1 bottle gin

Pick the sloes when soft (usually after one or two frosts). Prick all over with a fine skewer or darning needle, and place in wide-necked jars with the sugar and almond essence or flaked almonds. Pour over the gin and cover the jars. Shake and turn the bottles every day. This gin may be strained and drunk at Christmas, but like all this type of drink, improves with keeping. Some people say sloe gin should be kept for at least a year before tasting and that keeping for seven years will give you a really marvellous drink.

Prunus spinosa

WATERCRESS

There is still plenty of watercress growing wild in streams, but pick with caution these days as there could be pollution from fertilisers and pesticides. Avoid picking, too, from stagnant water or streams which run through fields where sheep are grazing, as the stems of the watercress could contain eggs of the liver fluke which attacks both human beings and sheep.

Plants are at their best when the leaves have a slightly bronze sheen. Wash them well before use. Watercress was valued for its anti-scorbutic properties and, with scurvy grass and Seville orange juice, was once sold as 'spring juices' for the treatment of scurvy. It is high in vitamin C content and a promotion for watercress a few years ago hinted strongly that it could have aphrodisiac properties! It was long used, too, as a cure for baldness, the juice being rubbed on the scalp to promote hair growth.

With all these virtues, it is not surprising that at least as early as the beginning of the 19th century it was 'cultivated to supply the London markets'.

CUCUMBER AND WATERCRESS SUMMER SOUP

600 ml (1 pt) chicken stock
2 large cucumbers, peeled and chopped
30 g (2 tbsp) mixed chopped onion, chives and parsley
Bunch watercress, chopped
30 g (2 tbsp) lemon juice
120 g (4 oz) natural yoghurt

Put the stock, cucumbers, herbs and watercress in a pan and simmer together until tender. When cold, liquidise or press through a sieve and add the lemon juice and yoghurt, mixing well. Season to taste with salt and pepper. Leave to chill. Serve decorated with a swirl of yoghurt, watercress leaves and very thin slices of cucumber.
Serves 4

HOT WATERCRESS SOUP

1 large bunch watercress
225 g (8 oz) leeks (white parts only)
225 g (8 oz) ripe tomatoes
Sprinkling celery seeds
1 litre (1¾ pt) tomato juice
Dash Worcestershire sauce
Salt and pepper

Wash and chop the watercress, reserving a few leaves for garnish. Chop the leeks and unpeeled tomatoes. Heat about 150 ml (¼ pt) of the tomato juice in a pan and simmer the leeks until soft, then add the watercress, celery seeds and chopped tomatoes. Simmer for 5 minutes, then add the rest of the tomato juice and Worcestershire sauce. Go on cooking until all the vegetables are tender, then sieve or blend until smooth. Taste and add salt and pepper. Reheat, pour into warmed bowls and decorate each with a swirl of cream or plain yoghurt and a few watercress leaves.
Serves 4–6

Rorippa nasturtium-aquaticum

OLD ENGLISH KEDGEREE

150 g (6 oz) long-grain rice
225 g (8 oz) cooked smoked haddock (or other smoked fish), without bone or skin
50 g (2 oz) butter
3 eggs, hard-boiled and shelled
Pepper
75 ml ($\frac{1}{8}$ pt) single cream
Chopped watercress

Boil about 850 ml (1$\frac{1}{4}$ pt) salted water in a large pan and drop in the rice. Cook until just tender, drain and run cold water through to separate the grains. Shake well in the colander. Chop the fish and the white of egg. Melt the butter in a pan, add the rice and a little pepper and stir to heat through. Add the chopped fish and egg white, then the cream and stir until hot (do not boil). Have ready the egg yolks and the watercress, chopped. Put the rice and fish in a heated dish and sprinkled with the yolks and watercress. Serve for breakfast with hot buttered toast.
Serves 4

WATERCRESS BUTTER

2 large handfuls of watercress
100 g (4 oz) butter
Squeeze of lemon juice
Salt and pepper

Pick off all the leaves, wash them and dry thoroughly. Chop up very finely indeed, slightly soften the butter and work the watercress and butter thoroughly together. Add the lemon juice and seasoning and work in. Chill the butter and either use pats on cooked fish or meat or spread on sandwiches (good in egg or chicken sandwiches).

WATERCRESS SAUCE FOR WHITE FISH

Large handful of watercress
300 ml ($\frac{1}{2}$ pt) mixed milk and fish stock
15 g (1 tbsp) butter
15 g (1 tbsp) flour
Salt and pepper to taste
15 g (1 tbsp) double cream

Strip off the watercress leaves. Put the stalks in the milk and stock and simmer. Meanwhile, chop the washed leaves finely. Melt the butter in a small pan, stir in the flour and cook for a few minutes. Strain the milk and stock over and cook together until smooth and creamy. Add the chopped watercress, taste and add a little salt and pepper if needed. Just before serving, mix in the cream, and reheat, being careful not to boil.

WATERCRESS SALADS

Watercress, orange segments, chopped celery, with oil and vinegar dressing – good with roast duck or game.
Watercress with sour cream. Wash watercress and discard coarse stems. Put in a bowl in iced water to chill. Mix a dressing as follows: 300 ml ($\frac{1}{2}$ pt) sour cream, 15 ml (1 tbsp) lemon juice, salt and pepper to taste, 2.5 g ($\frac{1}{2}$ tsp) celery seeds. Mix dressing ingredients together. Drain and dry the watercress and pour dressing over just before serving.
Mushroom salad with watercress. Choose small, white button mushrooms. Wipe and slice, without peeling and put in a bowl with oil and vinegar dressing. Leave to marinate in the refrigerator, stirring from time to time. Wash and dry some watercress, discarding tough stems. Put in a bowl and when ready to serve, put the drained mushrooms in the middle. Sprinkle the dressing over mushrooms and watercress.
Tomato and watercress salad. 450 g (1 lb) tomatoes, skinned and sliced, $\frac{1}{2}$ unpeeled cucumber, cubed, 1 medium onion, finely chopped, large handful watercress (stalks removed, leaves coarsely chopped), salad oil and lemon juice (4 parts oil to 2 of juice), dash Tabasco sauce. Mix together the tomatoes, cucumber, onion and watercress. In another bowl, mix the oil, lemon juice and Tabasco sauce. Pour dressing over the salad and toss before serving.

Rosa canina

WILD ROSE

Beware of the dog rose in June,
for if it be brought too near
the eyes it produceth blindness
and violent earache if it
should touch the ear.
(16th-century saying)

However that may be, one of the loveliest sights in our hedgerows is a mass of wild roses in full bloom, ranging from white to deepest shell pink. Nibble a petal or two as you walk along the lanes – the delicate taste gives you just a hint of sweetness and rose perfume which is infinitely subtle. There are many ways in which you can use rose petals, but do gather them when the fruit has had a chance to 'set' and they are just on the point of falling of their own accord.

In the past, the leaves were dried and infused to make a kind of herb tea – I must confess that I have not tried this, but it could be one to experiment with.

The other great gift of the wild rose is its hips – much liked by pheasants and a rich source of vitamin C, as witnessed by wartime rosehip syrup. There are a number of recipes for hips, too – these are best gathered when very ripe, but again, remember the birds and do not over-pick.

A little-quoted extract from Shakespeare (*Timon of Athens*) shows that rose hips were used in the 16th century, and pays tribute to nature's bounty:

Why should you want? Behold the
earth hath roots;
Within this mile break forth a hundred
springs;
The oaks bear mast, the briers scarlet
hips;
The bounteous housewife nature, on
each bush
Lays her full mess before you.

BLUSHING APPLES
450 g (1 lb) ripe rose hips
225 g (8 oz) sugar
Grated zest of $\frac{1}{2}$ lemon
450 g (1 lb) cooking apples
Whites of 2 eggs
100 g (4 oz) caster sugar
Vanilla essence

Halve the rose hips and remove all seeds and hairs (it is very important to get rid of the latter, even though this is a sticky job). Leave to soak overnight in a little water. Put the hips and water in a pan, with 100 g (4 oz) sugar and lemon zest. Simmer, adding more water if the rosehips become too stiff and dry.

Peel, core and chop the apples and put to cook in another pan with 100 g (4 oz) sugar.

Butter a dish lightly, and when the apples are cooked and soft, put them in. When the hips are soft, press them through a sieve (or purée in a blender) and spread over the apples.

Whisk the egg whites until stiff enough to stand in peaks. Add half the caster sugar and beat again until very thick. Fold in the rest of the caster sugar and two or three drops of vanilla essence. Pipe in whirls or drop from a spoon on top of the rosehip mixture and place in a cool oven (120°C/250°F/Gas $\frac{1}{2}$) for at least an hour or until cooked. Remove from oven and serve the dish cold with sponge finger biscuits and thin cream.
Serves 4

HIP TEA

Cut the tops and tails off the hips, split in half and remove the seeds and hairs. Spread them on a baking sheet covered with foil and place in a low oven until they are completely dry. Grind in a coffee grinder and store in a jar. To make the tea, use about 8 g/1 heaped tsp per cup, pour boiling water over and infuse for 5 minutes or more. Strain and sweeten if liked with a little honey.

HIP SYRUP

1 kg (2.2 lb) rose hips
3 litres (5¼ pt) water
Sugar

Clean the rose hips of seeds and hairs and chop them finely. Boil the water, drop in the hips and simmer for 15 minutes. Strain the juice and measure and to each 600 ml (1 pt) of juice add 275 g (10 oz) of sugar, making sure it is dissolved. Pour into warmed Kilner or other bottling jars (not too full), cover and cool. Prepare a large pan by putting a folded cloth in the bottom and place the jars on it. Loosen the tops very slightly, pour in enough water to come to the shoulders of the jars and bring the pan very slowly to simmering point. Simmer for about half an hour. Remove jars from the pan, placing them on a clean dry cloth on the worktop, and tighten up the bottle tops. Leave to cool.

PETAL ICE CREAM

300 ml (1 cup) rose petals
60 ml (4 tbsp) Rosé wine
25 g (1½ tbsp) caster sugar
Vanilla ice cream

Discard the white parts of the petals and blend the rest thoroughly with the wine and sugar. Take enough vanilla ice cream for four people, slightly soften it and thoroughly blend in the petal and wine mixture. Refreeze and serve. Serves 4

MEDIEVAL PRESERVED ROSES

Wild rose petals
Caster sugar

Pick off all the white bits from the petals. Pound the petals in a mortar or blend very well. To every 25 g (1 oz) of petals add 75 g (3 oz) of sugar, blending or pounding together until completely amalgamated. Place in little sterile pots and seal closely. Use quickly.

ROSE PETAL CONSERVE

300 ml (½ pt) water
325 g (12 oz) sugar
300 ml (½ pt) measure of rose petals
5 ml (1 tsp) lemon juice

Put sugar and water in a pan and boil together until the mixture starts to thicken. Discard the white parts of the rose petals and add rest to the syrup with the lemon juice. Simmer together gently for about an hour, stirring often. Pour into small sterile jars, cool and cover in the usual way.

ROSE PETAL SANDWICHES

Thin cut white bread
Butter
Cream cheese
Milk or cream
Wild rose petals
Caster sugar
(Proportions: 50 g/2 oz cream cheese to 25 g/1 oz petals, 5 g/1 tsp sugar, 10 ml/2 tsp cream or milk)

Thinly butter slices of white bread and cut out using a pastry cutter or tumbler about 7 cm (3 in) in diameter (or, if you have one, use a heart-shaped cutter).

Mix the cream cheese with a few drops of milk. Pick the white points off the rose petals and discard them. Finely chop the petals and mix with the sugar, then mix with the cream cheese.

Spread half the bread shapes with the cheese and rose petal mixture and place the other slices on top. If circular shapes, cut across the diameter.

Arrange the sandwiches on a small round plate to resemble a rose, leaving a space in the centre. Arrange one or two fresh flowers and leaves in the middle.

Rosa canina

Rubus fruticosus

BLACKBERRY

He who sows brambles must not go barefoot.
(Spanish saying)

There can not be many of us who have not rambled along fields and hedgerows in the late sunshine, picking the shining fruit of the bramble, staining hands and mouths purple and scratching legs and arms in efforts to reach even bigger and better blackberries.

There are many culinary uses for blackberries, the biggest and earliest to ripen being the best to eat as a dessert with the addition only of a little sugar and cream.

After the beginning of October, the fruits are not much use, so make the most of the rich harvest during August and September. When I was a child, I was told that late in the year, the blackberries belonged to the devil (or he had spat on them) and it was very unlucky to pick them – and neither I nor my friends would touch one!

There is a quaint legend about the origins of the bramble, quoted in *The Flowers of Shakespeare* by Doris Hunt (Webb & Bower): 'The cormorant was once a wool merchant. He entered into partnership with the bramble and the bat, and they freighted a large ship with wool; she was wrecked and the firm became bankrupt. Since that disaster the bat skulks about till midnight to avoid his creditors, the cormorant is forever diving into the deep to discover its foundered vessel while the bramble seizes hold of every passing sheep to make up his loss by stealing the wool.'

PORK WITH SWEET-AND-SOUR BRAMBLE SAUCE

675 g (1½ lb) lean cooked pork, cubed
Batter to coat (made from 100 g/4 oz self-raising flour, 2.5 g/½ tsp salt, sprinkling of pepper, about 120 ml(8 tbsp) water
225 g (8 oz) blackberries
100 g (4 oz) soft brown sugar
150 ml (¼ pt) malt vinegar
30 g (2 tbsp) cornflour
300 ml (½ pt) cold water

Cut the cooked pork into 2.5 cm (1-in) cubes. Make up the batter and leave in the refrigerator while making the bramble sauce. Simmer the blackberries, sugar and vinegar until the berries are soft, mashing with a wooden spoon from time to time. Blend the cornflour in a bowl with a little of the water, add the rest of the water to the blackberries and vinegar. Strain the blackberry mixture over the cornflour, discard the berries and return the cornflour mixture to the pan. Stir over a low heat until it thickens. Shake the cubed pork in a bag with a little seasoned flour to coat. Dip in the batter and deep fry in hot fat until the batter is crisp and the pork heated through. Drain on kitchen paper and put on a hot dish. Serve with the sauce in a separate bowl accompanied by rice and a green salad.
Serves 4

Rubus fruticosus

MELON AND BLACKBERRY STARTER
Medium size honeydew melon
225 g (8 oz) ripe blackberries
25 g (1 oz) sugar
15 ml (1 tbsp) kirsch

Cut the top off the melon and scoop out the seeds. Using a melon baller if you have one, cut out the flesh into balls (or cut out and cut into cubes if you have no baller). Put the melon flesh in a bowl in the refrigerator, with the melon shell.

Lightly stew the berries with the sugar. Cool. Mix the melon, blackberries and kirsch together and put back into the melon shell. Chill until needed.
Serves 4

SCALDBERRY CHUTNEY
225 g ($\frac{1}{2}$ lb) blackberries
225 g ($\frac{1}{2}$ lb) cooking apples, peeled and chopped
1 large onion, finely chopped
2 cloves garlic, finely chopped
13 mm ($\frac{1}{2}$-in) fresh ginger root, peeled and finely chopped
300 ml ($\frac{1}{2}$ pt) red wine vinegar
100 g (4 oz) soft dark brown sugar
100 g (4 oz) sultanas
5 g (1 tsp) salt
2.5 g ($\frac{1}{2}$ tsp) ground cinnamon
2.5 g ($\frac{1}{2}$ tsp) ground nutmeg
5 g (1 tsp) coriander seeds, ground

Put all the ingredients together in an aluminium saucepan, bring to the boil, then simmer gently for 2 to 2$\frac{1}{2}$ hours or until the berries are tender. Put into warmed jars and seal in the usual way. This may be used at once, but improves if kept for a couple of weeks.

BUMBLEKITE DELIGHTS
450 g (1 lb) ripe, juicy blackberries
50 g (2 oz) sugar
450 ml ($\frac{3}{4}$ pt) whipping cream
205 g (7$\frac{1}{2}$ oz) evaporated milk
45 ml (3 tbsp) liqueur (Benedictine, Kirsch or other)
2 sachets gelatine
Hot water

Press the blackberries through a sieve to extract the purée and leave behind the seeds. Add the sugar. Whip the cream, reserving a little for decoration, and whip in the evaporated milk. Stir into the blackberry and sugar purée and add the liqueur.

Into 60 ml (4 tbsp) hot water stir the gelatine. Dissolve completely, cool and mix thoroughly into the blackberry mixture.

Put into small cases or pots and allow to set. Decorate each with some cream and a fresh blackberry. Makes 8–10 pots

MELBOURNE PANCAKES
100 g (4 oz) plain flour
25 g (1 oz) caster sugar
2 eggs
300 ml ($\frac{1}{2}$ pt) milk
Lard or other fat for frying
450 g (1 lb) very ripe blackberries
Sugar

Put the flour and sugar in a bowl, make a well in the centre and break in the eggs. Mixing from the middle, work in the flour and half the milk, a little at a time. Beat well, then add the rest of the milk and mix.

Melt a little lard or fat in a 20-cm (8-in) frying pan and when smoking pour in a little batter. Cook until brown underneath, turn and cook the other side. As each is cooked, set aside. Have the blackberries ready, lightly crushed and sprinkled with more caster sugar. Layer the pancakes with the fruit and serve with whipped cream.

AUTUMN PUDDING
450 g (1 lb) blackberries
2 large cooking apples
225 g (8 oz) sugar
2.5 g ($\frac{1}{2}$ tsp) cinnamon
Thinly-sliced white bread
Butter

Take an 850 ml (1$\frac{1}{2}$ pt) pudding basin and butter lightly. Peel and core the apples and cut into thin slices. Put in a pan with sugar and cinnamon and stew lightly until the apples are tender but still in slices. Add the blackberries and cook for a minute or two until the juice starts to run. Take off the heat.

Butter the bread thinly and cut off the crusts. Line the basin with bread, leaving no gaps, butter side to the basin. Fill with the cool cooked blackberry and apple mixture. Cover with a bread 'lid' (which need not be buttered). Cover with foil or clingfilm and put a plate with a weight on top. Put in the refrigerator and leave for 24 hours. Turn out and serve with thin cream or cold custard.
Serves 4

BLACKBERRY WINE
3 kg (6 lb) blackberries
1.4 kg (3 lb) sugar
6 litres (10 pt) water
Wine yeast
Nutrient

Put the fruit in a plastic bucket or other wine-making vessel and crush well (a potato masher is useful for this). Boil the water and pour over the fruit, stir and leave to become lukewarm. Add the yeast and nutrient according to directions on the packet, then cover and leave for five days, stirring each day. Then strain over the sugar in another container and stir well to dissolve it. Pour into fermentation carboys reserving a little liquid for later 'topping up' (do not overfill) and fit an airlock. When the fermentation slackens, top up with the reserved liquid and replace the airlock. When clear, strain off and bottle. Bottles should be dark, as for red wine, so that the colour stays good.

BACARDI WITH BLACKBERRIES
Ripe blackberries
Bacardi

Crush some ripe blackberries and half-fill bottles with them. Fill up the bottles with Bacardi and screw on the tops. Leave to infuse for two or three weeks, shaking each day. Then filter off the Bacardi. This is delicious diluted with soda water and iced as an aperitif – I like it as a not-too-sweet liqueur with coffee, undiluted. Do not throw away the Bacardi-impregnated blackberries. Cooked with sugar and some sliced apples they make a delicious jam.

Bramble bush

BLACKBERRY SAUCE
450 g (1 lb) very ripe, juicy blackberries
Sugar
Apricot brandy

Press the raw blackberries through a sieve, add a little sugar and apricot brandy (or creme de menthe or other liqueur as preferred). Stir well together. Serve on plain ice cream.

BLACKBERRY SYRUP
Proportions as follows:
450 g (1 lb) ripe, juicy blackberries
450 g (1 lb) sugar
15 ml (1 tbsp) cold water
30 ml (2 tbsp) brandy

Stew the blackberries, sugar and water gently until the fruit is soft. Press the juice out through a nylon sieve, then put back in the pan and simmer for another 20 minutes, skimming from time to time. Take off the heat and add the brandy. When completely cold, bottle. This is delicious mixed with hot water, or iced with the addition of lemonade or soda. Or use it as a mixer that is slightly different with gin.

APPLE AND BLACKBERRY PRESERVE
2 kg (4 lb) apples
900 g (2 lb) blackberries
2 kg (4 lb) sugar

Put the blackberries in a pan with 450 g (1 lb) of the sugar and leave for at least 12 hours. Then put the pan on the heat and stew gently until the juice is extracted.

Peel, core and slice the apples, put into a large pan and strain the blackberry juice over them. Add the rest of the sugar and simmer gently for 45 to 60 minutes, skimming occasionally. Pour into clean jars, cover and store.

INVALID CREAM
This is one for people who like blackberries, but not the seeds!

900 g (2 lb) very ripe and juicy blackberries.

Put the berries either in a jelly bag, large square of cheesecloth or a big nylon sieve and squeeze or press so that the pulp collects in a basin held below. Leave in a warm place for at least two hours and it will set quite firmly and be the same consistency as junket. Serve with sponge finger biscuits and whipped or clotted cream. No sugar should be necessary.
Serves 2–4

SCALDBERRY FOOL
To make a very simple fool, use the pulp obtained as described above, mixed with whipped cream and chilled in individual glasses. The delicate purple colour looks most attractive served in glass rather than china.

CRUNCH MUESLI PUDDING
225 g (8 oz) blackberries
1 kg (2 lb) cooking apples, peeled, cored and sliced
6 whole cloves
75 ml ($\frac{1}{8}$ pt) water
2 large eggs
45 g (3 tbsp) cornflour
45 g (3 tbsp) golden syrup
450 ml ($\frac{3}{4}$ pt) milk
50 g (2 oz) butter
100 g (4 oz) muesli

Cook the blackberries, apples, cloves and water together until tender and put in an ovenproof dish.

Make a custard using the eggs, cornflour and 15 ml (1 tbsp) of the syrup, beating together in a pan. Stir in the milk and cook over a low heat, whisking all the time, until it thickens. Take off the heat and pour over the fruit.

Melt the rest of the syrup and butter together and stir in the muesli. Spread over the custard. Bake at 180°C/350°F (Gas 4) for 20 to 30 minutes (check the top is not burning). Serve hot or cold with single cream if liked. Serves 4–6

Rubus idaeus

WILD RASPBERRY

You will find this plant growing in woods and hedges, particularly in hilly country and, like the wild strawberry, the berries have a delicious slightly sharper flavour than the cultivated variety.

As a Victorian cookery writer puts it: 'The fruit, as presented by nature, is grateful to most palates, but sugar improves the flavour, and hence it is most esteemed when made into a sweetmeat'.

Raspberry leaf tea is recommended by some as an aid to slimming, and was traditionally drunk by pregnant women as it was thought to make childbirth easier.

MERINGUE NESTS
Whites of 4 large eggs
100 g (4 oz) caster sugar
325 g (12 oz) raspberries
150 ml ($\frac{1}{4}$ pt) double or whipping cream
Icing sugar to taste

Wipe a baking tray with a damp cloth and place on it a piece of greaseproof paper on which you have drawn four circles about 10-cm (4-in) in diameter.

Beat the egg whites until they stand in peaks. Add half the sugar and beat until the mixture is very thick. Fold in the rest of the sugar. Spread a layer of meringue on the circles, then mould a rim round each using a piping tube or spoon, leaving a depression in the centre. Cook in a cool oven (120°C/250°F/Gas $\frac{1}{2}$) for two hours or longer until the meringue is completely dry. Cool.

Mix the raspberries with the cream which has been stiffly whipped. If liked, mix in a little icing sugar. Pile the raspberry cream into the meringue nests to serve.
Serves 4

RASPBERRY TRIFLE
225 g (8 oz) raspberries
15 g (1 tbsp) sugar
Small bought jam Swiss roll or 4 small trifle sponges
30 ml (2 tbsp) sweet sherry
Small tin fruit salad
600 ml (1 pt) custard (either tinned or freshly made and cooled)
300 ml ($\frac{1}{2}$ pt) double or whipping cream
Few raspberries, angelica, blanched almonds, candied alexanders or other decorations

Lightly stew the raspberries with the sugar, crushing slightly, and leave to cool. Cut up the Swiss roll or trifle sponges and place in the bottom of the bowl in which the trifle will be served. Sprinkle with the sherry and the juice from the tin of fruit salad. Spread with the raspberries, then with the fruit salad. Pour the custard over, and then the cream, stiffly whipped. Leave for an hour or two in the refrigerator so the sherry and fruit juice soak thoroughly into the sponge. Just before serving, decorate to taste.
Serves 6

LEAF REFRESHER

Carefully dry wild raspberry leaves in a cool oven, or a warm, dry place, and store in a jar. To make a drink comforting for colds and influenza, pour boiling water over the leaves, leave to infuse and strain. Sweeten with honey. (Use 25 g/1 oz leaves to 600 ml/1 pint boiling water.) In summer, use the fresh leaves, add sugar and lemon or milk.

RASPBERRY SOUFFLÉ

225 g (8 oz) ripe raspberries
50 g (2 oz) caster sugar
50 g (2 oz) cornflour
150 ml ($\frac{1}{4}$ pt) whipping cream
4 eggs, separated
50 g (2 oz) stale cake crumbs (or white bread-crumbs)
15 g ($\frac{1}{2}$ oz) butter

Put the raspberries, sugar, cornflour and cream in a bowl and beat or blend to a pulp. Beat in the egg yolks and add the crumbs. Stiffly whip the egg whites and fold into the mixture. Prepare a mould or soufflé dish with a 'collar' of grease-proof paper and butter it well. Bake in a pre-heated oven at 190°C/375°F (Gas 5) for 30 to 45 minutes until risen and browned. Serve at once. Serves 4–6

MOUSSE

450 g (1 lb) ripe raspberries
75 g (3 oz) plain yoghurt, 50 g (2 oz) cottage cheese sieved and beaten together, or liquid-ised
2.5 ml ($\frac{1}{2}$ tsp) lemon juice
5 ml (1 tsp) clear honey
15 g (1 tbsp) powdered gelatine
Hot water
Whites of 2 eggs

Press the raspberries through a sieve to get rid of the seeds. Beat together the cottage cheese mix-ture, the lemon juice and honey and fold into the raspberry purée. Dissolve the gelatine in a little hot water and blend well with the raspberry mixture. Whip the egg whites until very stiff and fold into the mixture. Pour into a mould and leave in the refrigerator until set.   Serves 4

RASPBERRY VINEGAR

675 g (1$\frac{1}{2}$ lb) raspberries
850 ml (1$\frac{1}{2}$ pt) white wine vinegar
Sugar

Put 225 g (8 oz) of raspberries in a wide-necked jar and pour the vinegar over them. Leave to infuse in a warm place or on a sunny windowsill for three days. Strain through a nylon sieve, draining the fruit well without pressing it. Repeat with another 225 g (8 oz) of raspberries, then with the last 225 g (8 oz). Measure the liquid and to each 600 ml (1 pt) add 450 g (1 lb) sugar. Put into an aluminium saucepan and boil gently for 10 minutes, skimming off any scum. Leave to cool, then put in small bottles, ready for use. Dilute with soda water and add ice for a refresh-ing summer drink.

SHRUB

Pick as many raspberries as you can find and put in an earthenware bowl or casserole in a cool oven until the juice runs freely. Squeeze the juice lightly through a muslin cloth or jellybag and add sugar to taste. If the fruit is very ripe and sweet, you will not need much. To four parts of the sweetened juice add one part of brandy and stir well. Bottle and cork and store in a cool place. Delicious as a liqueur with coffee.

MILK SHAKE

For each glass:
150 ml ($\frac{1}{4}$ pt) milk
30 g (2 tbsp) fresh raspberry juice
5 ml (1 tsp) clear honey
5 g (1 tsp) chopped eau-de-cologne mint, lemon balm or other aromatic herb.

Mix ingredients together and whisk or blend. Leave to infuse at room temperature for an hour, strain. Place in a glass and chill in the re-frigerator. Decorate with a sprig of whatever herb was used.

FREEZER 'JAM'

Put equal quantities of sugar and berries in a heatproof bowl and leave in a cool oven until the sugar is dissolved. Stir well, cool and place in pots (do not overfill). Place in the freezer.

Rumex acetosa

SORREL

A type of dock, this plant is very similar to other members of its botanical family. However, you have only to nibble the edge of a leaf and taste its pleasant, lemony astringency to recognise it, and it is very common in fields and hedgerows. As the leaves come through early in spring, it can be picked at a time of year when other green flavourings and vegetables are scarce, though some writers warn that it should not be eaten too often. Sorrel is widely used in French cookery – a larger cultivated variety than the wild one.

SORREL SAUCE
25 g (1 oz) butter
15 g (½ oz) flour
600 ml (1 pt) stock (use chicken stock cube and
    water)
Small bayleaf
8 black peppercorns
2 good handfuls sorrel leaves
Salt and pepper

Melt the butter in a pan and stir in the flour. Cook for a few minutes then gradually add the stock, mixing all the time. Put in the bay leaf and peppercorns, then simmer slowly, stirring from time to time, for about 20 minutes. Remove bay leaf and peppercorns. Meanwhile, wash and pick over the sorrel, discarding stems. Chop and put in a saucepan without water (do not dry the leaves when you wash them) and cook until tender. Blend to a purée or press through a nylon sieve. Add to the white sauce, stir and cook for three or four minutes, stir in a small knob of butter, season and serve on poultry or fish.

SORREL AND SPINACH SALAD
100 g (4 oz) sorrel leaves
100 g (4 oz) spinach leaves
6 spring onions
Lemon juice
Vegetable oil
Salt and pepper
4 hardboiled eggs

Pick over and wash the sorrel and spinach leaves, discarding tough stems. Shred or tear the leaves into small pieces. Clean and chop the spring onions. Mix together in a bowl. Mix 15 ml (1 tbsp) oil with a little lemon juice, salt and pepper, pour over the salad and mix. Garnish with the shelled hardboiled eggs, cut into quarters lengthways. Serve as a starter with brown bread and butter. Serves 4

TUNA SALAD WITH SORREL
1 large or 2 small celeriacs
15 ml (1 tbsp) lemon juice
90 ml (6 tbsp) mayonnaise
150 g (6 oz) sorrel leaves
3 sticks celery
200 g (7 oz) tin tuna (or pink salmon if preferred)
100 g (4 oz) cooked red kidney beans

Peel the celeriac and cut into small cubes. Drop into boiling salted water with the lemon juice and cook until tender. Drain well. When cool, mix with the mayonnaise, finely chopped sorrel leaves, chopped celery, flaked fish and beans. Serve on a bed of shredded lettuce as a starter. Serves 4

Salicornia europaea

MARSH SAMPHIRE

Samphire or glasswort (as it was formerly used in the manufacture of glass) is common around the shores of Europe, Asia, Africa and America 'wherever the shores are flat and oozy', as an old herbal remarks. This is certainly true, from my own experience of squelching round the mud flats at low tide, to find the most succulent specimens – though you can often pick smaller plants growing in the sand higher up. Tradition has it that it can be first picked on the longest day of the year, though in my area this is too early. It is certainly very prolific, and is said to be the first plant to establish itself where marshy land takes over from seashore. The best samphire is that which is washed by two tides a day.

If you cannot go picking for yourself, look out for it in fishmongers' shops, or round the coast, at cottage gateways, together with local cockles and crabs.

We find samphire one of the most delicious vegetables, both as a starter and an accompaniment to meat or fish. The tender young tips can be used raw in salads, and many people pickle it for winter use. I have kept it for several days in the refrigerator – never leave it in water, or it will quickly deteriorate. It needs very thorough washing to remove the mud and bits of seaweed, then it can either be trimmed of its roots, or cooked with the roots still on (if not too large). We have introduced many friends to samphire and all have enjoyed it – to our taste it is a delicacy on a par with asparagus.

SIMPLE SAMPHIRE STARTERS
Allow about 900 g (2 lb) of samphire for six people.
Wash and clean as described.

Hot
Drop the samphire into boiling unsalted water and cook for 15 to 20 minutes or until a little, tested, is tender when run through the teeth. Drain and serve with a small pot of melted butter for each person to dip it in.
Cold
Drain the cooked samphire and serve cold accompanied by French dressing, oil and vinegar or simply vinegar.

PICKLED SAMPHIRE
(an old Norfolk recipe)
Cut off the roots, wash well in salted water and pick clean. Put out of doors on a clean cloth to dry for 2 or 3 hours. Pack the samphire into a stone jar with a few spices – ginger, whole peppers, cloves – now and then between the layers. Pack the samphire tightly as it sinks down, then fill up with vinegar. Set the jar, covered with a saucer, in a large saucepan of warm water and bring to the boil. Let it simmer until the samphire can easily be stripped off the stalks. Take off the heat, and when cold, cover and tie down.

Salicornia europaea

CRAB CUSTARDS WITH SAMPHIRE
3 medium-sized dressed crabs
2 egg yolks
90 ml (6 tbsp) double cream
75 g (3 oz) soft tips of samphire
Salt and pepper

Scoop the crabmeat into a bowl and mash with a fork. Whip the egg yolks with the cream, season with pepper and salt. Cook the samphire tips for 2 minutes in boiling water. Mix together the ingredients and put into 4 buttered ramekin dishes. Bake in the oven at 190°C/375°F (Gas 5) for 20 to 30 minutes, until firm in the middle. Serve with fingers of brown buttered toast and extra cooked samphire if liked.
Serves 4 as a starter

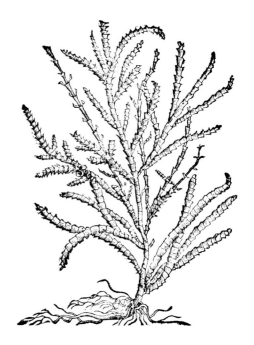

Glasswort

SPAGHETTI WITH COCKLES AND SAMPHIRE
450 g (1 lb) spaghetti (uncooked weight)
600 ml (1 pt) cockles (shelled weight)
450 g (1 lb) samphire
75 g (3 oz) butter
4 cloves garlic (or less or more to taste)
Lemon wedges

Drop the spaghetti into boiling salted water. While it is cooking, drain the cockles well, warm the butter in a pan, press the garlic and add the juice to the butter. Wash the samphire and snip off the tender tips. Heat the cockles through well in the garlic butter, add the samphire tips, continue to heat through. When the spaghetti is cooked, drain it and run cold water through to separate the strands. Mix the spaghetti into the hot butter with the cockles and samphire. Shake over the heat until piping hot, adding a little more butter if necessary. Garnish with lemon wedges. Serve as a light supper dish.
Serves 3–4

Snail Glasswort

Clean the mackerel, put inside each a little parsley, salt and pepper. Squeeze lemon juice over. Grill both sides until cooked through. Meanwhile, clean the samphire and drop into boiling unsalted water. Drain when cooked. Serve the mackerel garnished with the samphire over which the juices from cooking the mackerel have been poured. Offer wholemeal rolls and mixed salad with the mackerel.
Serves 4

MACKEREL WITH SAMPHIRE GARNISH
4 medium-sized mackerel
Parsley, salt, pepper, lemon
225 g (8 oz) samphire

102

ELDER TREE

You may shear your sheep
When the elder blossoms peep.
(Old Devonshire saying)

This unpretentious and usually small tree has long been highly regarded as a medicinal and culinary plant. When in flower, it appears to be covered in exquisite cream lace, and it is equally spectacular when the berry heads hang down in their rich black jet-bead ripeness.

In past ages all parts of the tree were used, from the bark and bud stage onwards. In fact, 19th-century books relate that 'the wood is commonly made into skewers for butchers, tops for angling rods and needles for weaving nets. The tree is also, as it were, a whole magazine of physic to rustic practitioners'. Beware, however, of sleeping under an elder tree – the same sources say that 'it has a narcotic smell – it is not prudent to sleep under its shade. In the flowering season it emits such a strong scent as will occasion violent pains in the heads of those who abide long near it.' And if you happened to be a turkey, it was said that the flowers could well prove fatal to you if eaten!

There is a great body of superstition connected with the elder, as with other white-flowered red-berried 'sacred' plants such as holly, rowan and hawthorn. Elders are said never to be struck by lightning, the weather never changes when it is in flower, its wood is 'warmer' than that of other trees, and it is very imprudent to prune it after nightfall. If you have a self-sown elder 'growing volunteer' in your garden, that is very lucky.

Gypsies think the tree is sacred and will not burn its wood as they claim that the elder can help to cure all the ills of mankind. If you believe in folklore, you should always tell the tree what you are doing and why if you need to cut its branches, or pick its flowers and berries.

Nowadays we use mainly the fruit and flowers; both are good for wines and drinks of various kinds, and the flowers go particularly well with gooseberries which are in season at the same time. The berries can be combined with apples or other wild berries to make a delicious variety of preserves and jellies – and if elderberry 'rob' or cordial does not actually cure your winter cough, it will certainly help to soothe it!

ELDERBERRY AND ORANGE WATER ICE
450 g (1 lb) elderberries
2 oranges
150 ml ($\frac{1}{4}$ pt) water
100 g (4 oz) sugar
2 egg whites

Put the berries in a pan with the grated rind and juice of the oranges. Add the water and simmer together until the elderberries are tender. Press through a sieve and return to pan with the sugar. Cook until the sugar is melted. Cool, then freeze until beginning to set. Whip the egg whites very stiffly. Whip the partly frozen elderberry mixture and fold in the egg whites. Re-freeze until firm.
Serves 4

'ROB' OF ELDERBERRIES
900 g (2 lb) elderberries, weighed after stripping
2.5 g (½ tsp) ground cinnamon
2.5 cm (1 in) fresh ginger, peeled and chopped
2.5 g (½ tsp) ground nutmeg
5 g (1 tsp) whole cloves
150 ml (¼ pt) water
2.5 g (½ tsp) crushed coriander seeds
Honey
Brandy

Boil all the ingredients except the honey and brandy together until the berries are soft, then strain. To each pint of juice add 225 g (8 oz) honey. Simmer for ten minutes. Cool slightly and add 150 ml (¼ pt) brandy to each 600 ml (1 pt). Bottle. Add hot or cold water as desired. This is a very soothing drink for colds and sore throats, but is equally good in the summer with soda and ice and a twist of lemon.

ELDERFLOWER FRITTERS
Coating batter
Elderflower heads
Deep fat for frying
Icing or caster sugar

Dip the elder heads into the batter and shake off the surplus. Plunge into hot fat and fry until golden. Sprinkle with icing or caster sugar and serve with cream.

ELDERFLOWER AND GOOSEBERRY FOOL
900 g (2 lb) gooseberries
225 g (8 oz) sugar
3 elderflower heads
600 ml (1 pt) made custard
300 ml (½ pt) double cream

Cook the first three ingredients together until the gooseberries are tender. Remove the elder heads, and cool the berries, then liquidise or press through a sieve. Mix with the cold custard and the cream which has been stiffly whipped. Chill in the refrigerator. When serving, decorate with a fresh elder flower. Garnish the edge with sponge finger biscuits if liked.
Serves 8 or more

PRESERVED ELDERBERRIES
900 g (2 lb) elderberries
100 g (4 oz) sugar

Use the jar in which you are going to store the berries. Layer the berries and sugar together to fill the jar. Cover with foil and put in a warm oven or stand in a pan of hot water until the juice begins to run. Seal the jar when hot and store, when cooled, in a cold place. Use as required with apples, in pies, or for ice cream or other recipes.

ELDERFLOWER FIZZER (non-alcoholic)
5 large heads elderflowers at their most perfumed
675 g (1½ lb) sugar
30 ml (2 tbsp) white wine vinegar
4.5 litres (1 gallon) water
2 large lemons

Shake the flowers free of insects and put in a large plastic container with the sugar, vinegar and water. Cut the lemons in half and squeeze the juice into the container, then add the squeezed halves too. Cover and leave in a warm place for a day, stirring occasionally. Strain through a piece of muslin or nylon sieve into clean, screw-top bottles. Screw the tops on tightly and leave for two or three days before drinking. The drink will be fizzy by this time and is best served chilled. Drink it within a week or ten days as it will not keep too long. One of the nicest of all summer drinks.

ELDERBERRY WINE
1.5 kg (3 lb) elderberries, stripped from stems
7 litres (1½ gallons) water
To each gallon of liquid allow the following:
450 g (1 lb) raisins
15 g (½ oz) ground ginger
6 cloves
2.5 g (½ tsp) all-purpose wine yeast
150 ml (¼ pt) brandy

Put the berries in a plastic container. Boil the water, pour it over the berries and leave to stand for a day. Bruise the berries and press the liquid through a plastic sieve or muslin cloth over another container.

Measure the juice and place in a preserving pan with all the other ingredients except the yeast and brandy. Boil gently for an hour, skimming when necessary. Put in a bucket and leave to stand until lukewarm, then stir in the yeast and cover. Leave for two weeks without disturbing. Strain, then add the brandy and pour into containers, corking tightly. Allow to rest for six months in a cool, dry place, then bottle off the wine, making sure the sediment remains behind. Cork and store. The wine can be drunk now, but is infinitely improved by keeping as long as your will power holds out!

'SANGRIA'
Try sangria made with your own elderberry wine rather than a 'Spanish red'!
Half a lemon and half an orange
6 small fresh peaches
1 litre (1¾ pt) elderberry wine
15 g (1 tbsp) sugar
300 ml (½ pt) soda water
Ice

Slice the fruit thinly, discarding stones and pips. Put the chilled wine into a jug which has been kept for an hour or two in the refrigerator. Put the fruit and sugar into the wine and stir well. Immediately before serving pour in the chilled soda water and ice cubes.
Makes 9–12 glasses

FRUIT KETCHUP
600 ml (1 pt) cider vinegar
450 g (1 lb) elderberries stripped from stems
10 g (2 tsp) demerara sugar
1 small onion, chopped
2.5 g (½ tsp) mace
2 cloves garlic, chopped
2.5 g (½ tsp) allspice
Piece fresh ginger root

Boil the elderberries and vinegar together and leave to infuse for a day. Press through a sieve and to the juice add the rest of the ingredients. Boil together, cool slightly, strain again and bottle. Use on fish or cooked meat.

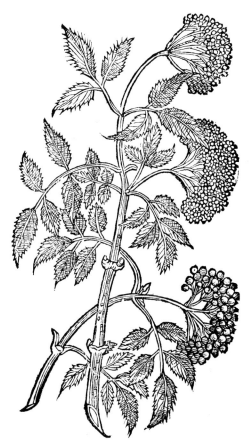

Elder with white berries

ELDERBERRY JAM
450 g (1 lb) elderberries, stripped from stems
225 g (8 oz) cooking apples, peeled and chopped
150 ml (¼ pt) water
Juice of 2 lemons
2 sprigs of lemon balm (if available)
675 g (1½ lb) sugar

Put all the ingredients into a pan and simmer until a small quantity, put on a plate, wrinkles when cold. Remove balm. Pour into hot sterilised jars and cover.

ELDERBERRY VINEGAR
325 g (¾ lb) elderberries
300 ml (½ pt) cider vinegar
2.5 g (½ tsp) sugar
Pinch mace
Small onion, chopped
2 cloves garlic, chopped
Few allspice

Boil together the elderberries and vinegar. Leave for a day and add the rest of the ingredients. Boil again, strain and bottle.

BROOM

Broom never seems to grow in isolated bushes, but in great masses, gleaming under the sun like heaps of gold when in flower. It is the old *planta genista* which, being adopted for the family crest, gave the Plantaganet line of kings their name.

If picking the flowers for salads and drinks be sure to pick the right variety of broom. The Spanish variety should not be used as it is poisonous. The leaves of this variety are thin and sharp like pine needles and it flowers later than the true broom. *S. scoparius* has more oval small leaves which are grouped in bunches of three. Flowering takes place from early April to June.

In past ages most parts of the broom were used – the twigs as brooms, as the name suggests; the bark fibres for cloth and paper; the green stem tips to flavour beer; the flowers in salads or wine and to dye cloth; and the seeds roasted to provide a drink. If you walk along by broom plants on a hot day in late summer, you will hear little explosions like the report of tiny rifles – it is the broom pods popping to release their seeds.

RABBIT IN BROOM SAUCE
4 young rabbit hind legs and 2 rabbit 'saddles'
1 small onion
2 carrots
1 stick celery
2.5 g ($\frac{1}{2}$ tsp) ground cloves
60 g (4 tbsp) chopped fresh parsley
Small bayleaf
Ground black pepper
50 g (2 oz) young broom flowers
3 or 4 threads saffron or 2.5 g ($\frac{1}{2}$ tsp) powdered
    saffron
Salt
25 g (1 oz) butter
15 g (1 tbsp) flour

Wipe the rabbit pieces and put in a pan with the onion, carrots and celery, chopped, the cloves, 15 g (1 tbsp) parsley, bayleaf, pepper, 30 g (2 tbsp) broom flowers, saffron and a sprinkling of salt.

Cover with water, stir well, put a lid on the pan and simmer for about three-quarters of an hour or until the rabbit is tender. Remove from the heat and take out the rabbit pieces with a draining spoon. Melt the butter, stir in the flour and cook for a minute or so. Gradually strain over it about 300 ml ($\frac{1}{2}$ pt) of the cooking liqueur (or a little more) and stir until it forms a thick sauce. Add the rest of the parsley and the broom flowers.

Take the rabbit meat off the bones in small, neat pieces, mix with the sauce and heat through. Serve with brown rice and a dressed green salad. Serves 4

Sarothamnus scoparius

ALEXANDERS

Very early in the year, near where I live a mile or two from the sea, the alexanders start pushing their vigorous dark green leaves through the earth in hedgerows and ditches. In this area, it is not a plant you can ignore. It grows so prolifically and is handsome in all its stages, with beautiful foliage, strange flower buds, striking umbels of flowers and seed heads of inky black seeds. A friend recently asked me to point out alexanders to her – now she says she can not get away from them!

The 19th-century herbalist and doctor, Thomas Green, remarks that it acquired its name of *Herba Alexandriana* in Germany because it was originally brought from Alexandria. It was certainly introduced into Britain by the Romans, and was used all over Europe as a salad or potherb. It is easy to see why, as it is one of the most versatile of plants, and the seeds were used medicinally to 'warm, strengthen and comfort the stomach, create an appetite, disperse wind, promote urine and the menses and give relief to the strangury'.

If you cultivate the plant (it seems to prefer coastal locations on the whole), you can draw up the earth round it and blanch and use as celery. My edition of Mrs Beeton's *Household Management* dated 1907 does, in fact, say that all the recipes she gives using celery were formerly made with alexanders.

On the whole, my favourite recipe for alexanders is the simplest – lightly boiled and then eaten as asparagus with butter. However, I have tried a number of recipes, all interesting. The flavour of the raw leaves I find too strong for my taste – you may disagree and think that, used sparingly, they add an interesting new ingredient to a spring salad. This distinctive flavour is retained in a subtle form in the candied stems and almost lost when the plant is cooked. The black seeds when chewed taste almost like liquorice – try them in the beef stew recipe below.

ALEXANDERS 'NATURE'
8 or 9 alexanders stems about 15 cm (6 in) for
  each serving
Melted butter
Ground black pepper and salt

You can use the stems as a starter, as you would asparagus, or as a vegetable accompaniment to meat or poultry.

Either pick the stems very young, in which case you will put your hand down as far into the grass as you can and pull the blanched, celery-like stems out, or pick at a later stage when the stems are fat and juicy and the flower buds are just going to open. In the former case, cut the blanched base off each stem to use (the upper stems may be candied – see page 110); in the latter, cut the stems into lengths, like asparagus and scrape off or peel the outer skin. Drop into boiling salted water and cook for seven or eight minutes until very tender. Serve with melted butter poured over and a light seasoning of pepper and salt.

Smyrnium olustratum

BEEF CASSEROLE WITH ALEXANDERS SEEDS

50 g (2 oz) margarine
1 large onion, finely chopped
2 cloves garlic, crushed
700 g (1½ lb) lean stewing beef, cubed
30 g (2 tbsp) flour
150 ml (¼ pt) stock
45 ml (3 tbsp) red wine
2 large green peppers, de-seeded and chopped
225 g (8 oz) ripe tomatoes, chopped
15 g (3 tsp) alexanders seeds, ground in mortar or
   crushed with a rolling pin
Salt and pepper
120 g (4 oz) carton yoghurt

Melt the margarine in a pan and fry the onion and garlic for a few minutes. Add the beef and continue to fry, stirring from time to time, until sealed and browned. Stir in the flour, mix and cook for two or three minutes, then pour in the stock and wine and add the peppers, tomatoes and alexanders seeds. Season with salt and pepper, cover and simmer for 1½ to 2 hours, until the meat is tender. Cool a little, stir in the yoghurt and reheat without boiling. Serve with rice or potatoes and any green vegetable.
Serves 4

CROQUETTES

225 g (8 oz) white base part of alexanders stems
   (weighed after trimming and cleaning)
300 ml (½ pt) chicken stock
25 g (1 oz) flour
Small onion, finely chopped
150 ml (¼ pt) milk
2 eggs
Breadcrumbs
Fat for frying

Cook the alexanders in the stock (or salt water if you prefer) until tender but still slightly crisp. Drain and chop finely. Cook the onion for a short time in the butter, stir in the flour and blend well. Gradually add the milk (off the heat), return to heat and blend until it begins to thicken. Season to taste, add the alexanders and cook together, stirring, for about 10 minutes. Cool a little, then add the beaten yolk of one egg and cook for a further minute or two. Spread the mixture on a plate to cool. Beat the remaining egg and white to use as coating. Form the mixture into croquettes about the size of an egg, roll in the beaten egg, then the breadcrumbs. Fry in a mixture of oil and butter until all sides are crisp. This is rather a fiddly recipe but the resulting croquettes, with their crisp outsides and creamy subtly-flavoured centres make it worth doing. Very good with cold meats or poultry.
Serves 4

STEM CANDY

Cut thick alexanders stalks into sections 12–15 cm (5–6 in) long. Pour boiling water over them, renewing it until the outer fibres of the stems soften. Drop the stems into ice cold water, then peel off the fibres.

Mix equal quantities of sugar and warm water to dissolve the sugar. Cool and pour over the stems, leaving for 24 hours. Pour off the syrup, leaving the stems in the bowl, and boil it until it registers 120°C/225°F on a sugar thermometer. Pour over the stems and leave for a day. Repeat this procedure for another two days.

On the following day, put the stems and sugar syrup, by now reduced, in a pan, bring to the boil, then take off the heat. When cold, strain off the syrup (this can form the basis for an interesting lemonade). Put the sugar-impregnated pieces of stem on a piece of aluminium foil dusted with icing sugar and sprinkle well with icing sugar. (Alternatively, put in a polythene bag with icing sugar and shake thoroughly.)

Put in a very low oven until dry and store in airtight jars.

CABBAGE SALAD

225 g (8 oz) crisp white cabbage, finely
100 g (4 oz) shelled walnuts, coarsely chopped
1 eating apple, cored and chopped
15 g (1 tbsp) alexanders leaves, finely chopped
Salt and pepper to taste
60 ml (4 tbsp) mayonnaise

Mix all the ingredients together and chill before serving.
Serves 4

Sorbus aucuparia

ROWAN or MOUNTAIN ASH

You will find rowan trees all over the place – but they are more likely to grow wild in woods, rocky places and on mountains. Elsewhere, they are cultivated as a popular garden tree – they are attractive in both blossom and bright red berry stage, the trees do not grow too large and they attract birds to feed on the fruit.

From the time of the Druids on, the rowan was regarded as a magic tree, with strong powers against witches. One planted near your door protects your house from evil, so it was said. Often a stump of rowan is to be found in old burial grounds and near the circles of Druid temples where sacred rites were performed.

There are many interesting customs connected with rowans, recorded in old books and proceedings of such bodies as the Folk-lore society. In the north, dairy maids used to drive the cattle to summer pastures with a rod of rowan and in parts of Scotland the local people would make a rowan-wood hoop and 'cause all the sheep and lambs to pass through it'. As late as the beginning of this century, countrywomen in the west of England would make a cross on each pot of preserve or jelly to stop it shrinking and store the jars with a rowan or hazel stick to prevent the fairies from stealing them.

The bright red of the berries clearly had much to do with the superstitions attaching to the rowan – red is traditionally a colour which repels evil, so it is said.

Used in cooking, you will find the berries sour and astringent, but giving a unique flavour to jellies, puddings and wine. The jelly is particularly good with rich meats or game and it is well worth making a few pots. Try it with turkey too, in place of cranberry jelly or sauce.

AUTUMN SEMOLINA
450 g (1 lb) rowan berries
450 g (1 lb) cooking apples
225 g (8 oz) blackberries or elderberries
600 ml (1 pt) water
100 g (4 oz) sugar
30 g (2 tbsp) semolina
15 g (1 tbsp) cornflour

Put the rowan berries, chopped cooking apples, blackberries or elderberries and water in a pan and cook together until soft. Squeeze the fruit through a piece of cheesecloth or muslin and measure the juice. Make up to just over 1 litre (2 pt) with water and return to the pan with the sugar. Bring to the boil, add the semolina and simmer for 10 to 15 minutes. Taste and add a little more sugar if preferred sweet. Take off the heat. Mix the cornflour with a little water, stir into the semolina and bring to the boil again. Pouring into a serving dish, cool and chill. Serve with plenty of lightly whipped cream and sponge finger biscuits.
Serves 4–6

ROWAN BRANDY

Large handful rowan berries stripped from stem
600 ml (1 pt) brandy
600 ml (1 pt) sugar syrup made from 1 part sugar
    to 1 part water.

Leave the berries on a plate in a warm place for
several days until they become shrivelled. Put in
a bottle with the brandy and leave for a fortnight,
turning the bottle frequently. Strain out the
berries and mix the brandy well with the syrup
which has been slightly warmed. Bottle. This is a
sweet liqueur very pleasant with black coffee. It
can be made sweeter or less so by adjusting the
sweetness of the syrup. If you make a little extra
syrup, you can boil the brandied rowan berries in
this, then spread on a piece of foil and dry in a
low oven. Sprinkled with icing sugar, they make
an unusual 'nibble'.

ROWAN JELLY

450 g (1 lb) ripe rowan berries
450 g (1 lb) cooking apples
600 ml (1 pt) water
Sugar

Put the rowan berries in a pan with the apples,
wiped and roughly chopped, but not peeled or
cored, and the water. Simmer together until soft
then put in a jelly bag or piece of cheesecloth or
muslin tied together at the corners and leave to
drip into a bowl overnight. For a very clear jelly,
use this juice only for the next stage, but if you
do not mind a slightly cloudy jelly, squeeze the
bag to extract more juice.

Measure the juice, and to each 600 ml (1 pt)
add 450 g (1 lb) sugar. Bring to the boil, skim,
then simmer, skimming from time to time, until
a little put on a saucer in a cool place wrinkles
when tested. Pour into clean warmed jars and
seal.

Wild ash

Sorbus aucuparia

CHICKWEED

This little, unobtrusive plant grows all over the place, in the hedgerows, neglected corner of the garden, in fields after the harvest. It is at its best in spring and autumn and is tender and delicate, so that stems as well as leaves may be used. Its flowers are minute white stars and quite unobtrusive. It has long been used as a food for humans and of course for cage birds and poultry and an old herbal states that 'when boiled it exactly resembles spinach'. It certainly has the same 'earthy' taste, which may or may not appeal to you, and it can be used in soup, or as an addition to salad or as a vegetable in its own right. The easiest way to harvest it is to snip it off with scissors rather than pulling it up by the roots.

POTATO SALAD WITH CHICKWEED
450 g (1 lb) cooked new potatoes, diced
30 ml (2 tbsp) cream
Sprinkling salt
225 g (8 oz) tomatoes, finely sliced
3 sprigs parsley, finely chopped
Large handful chickweed (young tips and leaves, no stalks)
Oil and vinegar dressing

Mix the potatoes with the cream and a little salt. Put a layer of tomatoes in a serving dish and cover with parsley. Cover with the potato mixture and over this put the chopped chickweed. Serve with the dressing in a separate bowl.
Serves 4

CHICKWEED PIE
225 g (8 oz) chickweed
10 g (2 tsp) salt
225 g (8 oz) shortcrust pastry
225 g (8 oz) cottage cheese
15 ml (1 tbsp) salad oil
2 eggs
Pepper to taste

Put the chopped chickweed in a bowl and sprinkle with the salt. Mix well by hand or with salad servers and leave for an hour or so.

Roll out the pastry very thinly and use about two-thirds to line a lightly greased baking tin about 25 cm (10 in) by 15 cm (6 in). Leave to chill in the refrigerator with the left-over piece.

Press the chickweed well in a sieve to remove any moisture and put in a bowl with the cheese, oil, one of the eggs, well beaten, and ground black pepper to taste. Mix together very well.

Put in the prepared tin, roll out the rest of the pastry and cover the mixture, damping and sealing the edges. Make several cuts in the top of the pie. Beat the other egg and use for brushing the top (or use milk if preferred).

Bake at 200°C/400°F (Gas 6) for about 45 minutes or until the pastry is browned and the chickweed cooked. Serve hot with chips and new young carrots or other vegetable to taste.
Serves 6

DANDELION

If the down flyeth off coltsfoot,
dandelion and thistles when there
is no winde, it is a signe of raine.
(Old weather lore)

Together with daisies, the dandelion is probably the plant we all remember most from our childhood, with its wide open, innocent golden flowers. It has a grand legend attached to it – that it was born from the dust raised by the sun chariot as it went across the sky. This is why its flowers open at dawn and close in the evening.

Most parts of the plant are edible, and old herbals state that 'early in the spring, while the leaves are hardly unfolded, they are not an unpleasant ingredient in salads. The French eat the roots, and the leaves, blanched, with bread and butter. On account of its powerful diuretic effects it obtained the vulgar name of Piss-a-bed. When a swarm of locusts had destroyed the harvest on the island of Minorca, many of the inhabitants subsisted upon this plant, and goats eat it and swine devour it greedily.'

I enjoy dishes made with the leaves, and the wine is worth drinking, but to call the beverage made with the roots 'coffee' is, I feel, the wrong name. It is a drink, but nothing like coffee and friends hold divided opinions as to whether they enjoy it or not. Have a go at one of the recipes below, which you may not have come across before.

DANDELION BRUNCH
For each serving:
3 rashers streaky bacon, without rind
1 large slice wholemeal bread
1 handful young dandelion leaves, washed, dried
  and roughly chopped

Cut the bacon into pieces and grill until cooked. Take out of the pan with a draining spoon and keep hot. Cut the bread into cubes and fry it in the bacon fat, adding a little butter or margarine if necessary. Toss so that all sides are crisp and browned. Take out of the pan and keep hot with the bacon. Toss the dandelion greens in the hot fat until coated and limp. Stir together the bacon, bread and dandelion leaves and serve in a warm bowl as a breakfast dish.

STEWED DANDELION LEAVES
450 g (1 lb) dandelion leaves
15 g ($\frac{1}{2}$ oz) butter
15 g (1 tbsp) flour
150 ml ($\frac{1}{4}$ pt) stock
30 ml (2 tbsp) single cream
Salt and pepper

Wash the leaves and leave in cold water in a cool place for an hour or two. Drain, just cover with boiling water, add a very small amount of salt, and simmer for 20 minutes, or until the leaves are tender. (The exact time will depend on how young they are.) Drain very well and chop finely. Melt the butter in a small pan and add the flour, cook for a minute or two, then gradually add the warm stock and cook until the mixture thickens. Add a spoonful or two of the sauce to the cream, mix and return all to the pan. Season to taste with salt and pepper. Mix in the dandelion leaves and heat through. Serve with poultry or veal. Serves 2–4

Thymus drucei

THYME

There are many varieties of thyme – most commonly you will find this low-growing plant with its pretty lilac flowers on dry, chalky soil in a sunny position – and its scent is delicious. It is another plant we probably have to thank the Romans for (our list is growing extensive) and it was used by both them and the Greeks in embalming and to fumigate clothes and rooms. Bees love it, and it is traditionally a 'fairy plant'.

Most of us have recited the familiar 'I know a bank whereon the wild thyme blows', from Shakespeare's *A Midsummer Night's Dream*, but did you know that it is used in an early 17th-century recipe for summoning up the fairies? This is no guarantee that it will work, of course, but these are the ingredients: 'A pint of sallet oyle and put it into a vial glasse; and first wash it with rosewater and marygolde water; the flowers to be gathered towards the east. Wash it till the oyle become white, then put into the glasse, and then put thereto the budds of hollyhocke, the flowers of marygolde, the flowers or toppes of wild thyme, the budds of young hazle and the thyme must be gathered neare the side of a hill where fairies use to be. Then all these put into the oyle and keepe it for thy use.'

However effective that recipe may be, thyme is a delicious herb for cooking, so if you find some, be sure to dry a good supply for winter use.

HONEYED POUSSINS WITH THYME
4 poussins
1 medium onion
100 g (4 oz) butter
20 g (4 tsp) fresh thyme, chopped
60 ml (4 tbsp) clear honey
Salt and pepper
150 ml ($\frac{1}{4}$ pt) single cream

Preheat the oven to 160°C/325°F (Gas 3). Peel and chop the onion and put a little in each chicken. Also put about 15 g ($\frac{1}{2}$ oz) butter and 2.5 g ($\frac{1}{2}$ tsp) thyme in each. Pour 15 ml (1 tbsp) honey over each, dot with 15 g ($\frac{1}{2}$ oz) butter and sprinkle with salt and pepper. Cover with foil and cook for 45 minutes, basting from time to time with the butter and honey mixture. Make sure the honey does not burn – if it seems too hot add a little water and lower the temperature slightly.

Remove foil, sprinkle with remaining herbs, baste again and cook for another 25 to 30 minutes, or until the poussins are brown and tender. Take out of the oven.

Remove the poussins and keep hot. Put the pan of juices and honey on a low heat and add the cream. Stir and cook together until completely blended and slightly thickened. Pour a little on the poussins and serve the rest in a sauceboat. Serve with new potatoes and a green vegetable. For a less special dish, use the same method with chicken pieces.
Serves 4

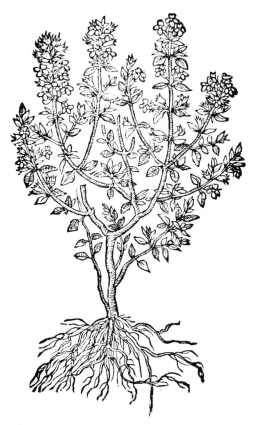

Common thyme

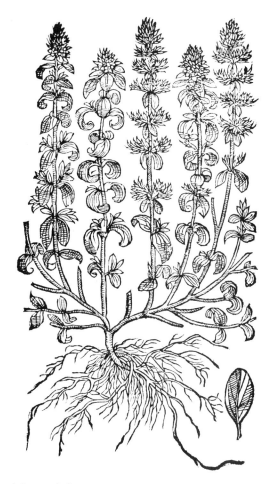

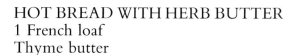

HOT BREAD WITH HERB BUTTER
1 French loaf
Thyme butter

Broad-leaved thyme

Make this in the same way as garlic bread, but using thyme butter in place of garlic and butter. To 100 g (4 oz) softened butter add the juice of half a lemon and 5–10 g (1–2 tsp) chopped fresh thyme, salt and ground black pepper. Mix thoroughly, tasting from time to time to check the strength of the herbs. Shape the butter into a roll about 2.5 cm (1 in) in diameter, wrap in foil and chill until needed or use for hot bread as follows.

Cut the loaf in sections about 8-cm (3-in) long, but do not cut it right through the bottom. Butter one cut side of each facing slice thickly with thyme butter. Press the loaf into shape again and wrap tightly in foil. Heat in a medium oven (180°C/350°F/Gas 4) for 20 minutes or so until the butter has melted and flavoured the bread and the crust is crisp. Serve very hot with soups, salads, etc.

CREAM OF RABBIT MOULDS
225 g (8 oz) raw rabbit meat
150 ml (¼ pt) thick white or béchamel sauce
1 small egg, beaten
2.5 g (½ tsp) fresh thyme, chopped
Salt and pepper

Mince the rabbit meat and pound in a mortar until smooth, or use a blender or food processor. Mix in the beaten egg and white sauce, the herbs and seasoning. Press into buttered small moulds or ramekin dishes and steam gently until firm. Serve with gravy and a green vegetable, or alone as a starter.
Serves 4

Tussilago farfara

COLTSFOOT

Another of those fascinating plants where the leaves and flowers appear separately. Early in spring come the cheerful little yellow flowers of the coltsfoot, with their neat scaly stems, then the large 'webbed' dramatic leaves follow in summer. These leaves are the basis of the British 'herb tobacco' and were formerly much used in coughs and consumptive complaints.

Do try the candy. It is an enjoyable way to soothe a cough.

COLTSFOOT CANDY
1 litre (1¾ pt) coltsfoot leaves
600 ml (1 pt) water
450 g (1 lb) sugar
450 g (1 lb) golden syrup
50 g (2 oz) butter
2.5 g (½ tsp) baking soda

Boil the washed coltsfoot leaves in the water, and strain off the liquid. Put the sugar, golden syrup and butter in a pan and add the liquid. Bring to the boil, stirring, then continue to boil until a little of the candy turns brittle when dropped into a bowl of cold water. Take off the heat and add the soda. Beat the mixture very well until it is almost stiff, then pour into a shallow, oiled baking tray. Allow to set, then break up into pieces and store in a jar.

COUGH MIXTURE
25 g (1 oz) dried coltsfoot leaves
600 ml (1 pt) water
15 ml (1 tbsp) honey (more if liked)

Boil the leaves in the water until it is reduced by half. Strain and add the honey, stirring until it is melted. Bottle. Drink, diluted with a little hot water, to ease a cough.

COLTSFOOT SPONGE
(Makes two 18-cm (7-in) cakes)
100 g (4 oz) butter
100 g (4 oz) caster sugar
2 eggs
100 g (4 oz) self-raising flour
Pinch salt
15 g (1 tbsp) coltsfoot petals, chopped
15 ml (1 tbsp) warm water
For the butter cream
100 g (4 oz) butter
100 g (4 oz) icing sugar
15 g (3 tsp) chopped coltsfoot petals
Coltsfoot flowers to decorate

Cream together the butter and caster sugar until pale and light. Add the eggs one at a time and beat thoroughly. Sift flour and salt together and mix into the butter, sugar and eggs. Stir in the petals, salt and warm water. Spread evenly into two cake tins which have been lightly buttered. Cook at 190°C/375°F (Gas 5) for about 20 minutes or until the cakes feel springy when pressed. Leave to cool in tins, then turn out onto a cake rack.

Meanwhile make butter cream by softening the butter and creaming it with the sugar. When smooth and light, stir in the coltsfoot petals.

When the cakes are cold, split and sandwich together with cream and pipe a central motif on top. Arrange a few coltsfoot flowers in the central motif as decoration.

Tussilago farfara

Urtica dioica

STINGING NETTLE

It nods and curtseys and recovers
When the wind blows above,
The nettle on the graves of lovers
That hanged themselves for love.
(A.E. Housman)

The agony of nettle stings, relieved by the application of dock leaves, is a memory of childhood. The Romans introduced the nettle – they are said to have whipped themselves with the plant to encourage good circulation! A leaf put upon the tongue and pressed against the roof of the mouth was an early remedy for nosebleeds and paralytic limbs are said to have been restored to their usual functions by stinging them with nettles. The plant is the food of several beautiful butterflies.

If you suffer from nettles in the garden, take heart. It is said that they grow particularly well in strong, fertile soil. To use as food, they should be gathered young and tender – but even then you will need good strong gloves to pick the young shoots. After being cut back in the summer, you may get a late year crop of shoots in autumn or fall for the recipes we suggest. Do not worry about being stung as you eat the soup! The herbalist John Gerard remarks that when boiled, the nettle 'stingeth not at all'.

POACHED EGGS WITH NETTLE PURÉE
225 g (8 oz) nettles, weighed after removing tough stalks
Salt and pepper
30 ml (2 tbsp) double cream
15 g ($\frac{1}{2}$ oz) butter
2 eggs
2 slices hot buttered wholemeal toast

Boil a little salted water and drop in the washed and finely chopped nettles. Simmer until they are soft. Drain very well, pressing out all the water with a spoon. Stir in the butter and cream and season to taste. Keep hot. Poach the eggs and prepare the buttered toast. Fluff up the nettle purée and divide between the two pieces of toast. Put a poached egg on top of each and serve at once.
Serves 2

FISHY NETTLE SOUP
225 g (8 oz) nettles, weighed after removing tough stalks
300 ml ($\frac{1}{2}$ pt) milk
450 ml ($\frac{3}{4}$ pt) water
1 chicken stock cube
1 bouquet garni
1 large onion finely chopped
450 g (1 lb) potatoes, peeled and diced
Salt and pepper
600 ml (1 pt) shrimps in the shell or 100 g (4 oz) shelled shrimps

Roughly chop the nettles, then put all the ingredients except the shrimps into a pan and simmer together until the nettles and potatoes are tender. Press through a sieve or liquidise, return to the pan and stir in the shelled shrimps. Heat through. Pour into warmed bowls and add a swirl of cream to each if liked.
Serves 4

Urtica dioica

Vaccinium myrtillus

BILBERRY

The small, unassuming bilberry plant thrives on moorland and sandy and acid soils in heath and woods – and produces one of the most delicious of wild berries. A larger variety grows in the eastern parts of America where it is equally enjoyed. The berry has a rich, dark blue bloom, very like the sloe in colour, and is slightly flattened at one side. Its juice gives a very deep purple stain which was once used as a dye. Eat with thick or clotted cream or milk, make them into tarts and jellies, pancakes or pies and, if you can find enough, try them as a wine. It is said to have been added to whisky in the past 'to give it a relish to strangers'. In Ireland, there has been a revival of 'Fraughan Sunday' (fraughan being the Irish name for bilberries, as blaeberries is in Scotland and blueberries in America) – a Sunday in August when bilberries were traditionally picked and a good time had by all!

PICKLED BILBERRIES
Bilberries
White wine vinegar
Sugar
Cayenne pepper

Pick over the bilberries, which should not be too ripe. Put them into clean, dry jars. To each 600 ml (1 pt) vinegar add 225 g (8 oz) sugar and a little cayenne pepper. Boil the mixture, skim well and simmer for a few minutes. Cool and when cold, pour over the bilberries and seal the jars in the usual way.

DRIED BILBERRIES
If you find a lot of bilberries, you could dry some and use as you would currants. Spread the berries in a tray, lightly covered with greaseproof paper, in a warm airing cupboard for a week or more until dry, or for a shorter time in a very cool oven. Store in jars.

BILBERRY WARMER
To each 450 g (1 lb) berries, add 50 g (2 oz) sugar and 150 ml ($\frac{1}{4}$ pt) water. Simmer until soft, then strain off the juice. Add a little cinnamon to taste and drink hot.

BILBERRY CRUMBLE
450 g (1 lb) bilberries
1 medium cooking apple, peeled and thinly sliced
15 g (1 tbsp) granulated sugar
75 g (3 oz) plain flour
2.5 g ($\frac{1}{2}$ tsp) ground cinnamon
50 g (2 oz) margarine or lard (or a mixture)
75 g (3 oz) brown sugar

Put the bilberries, apples and sugar, mixed together into a baking dish.

Mix together the flour and cinnamon and rub in the fat with the finger tips (or by machine) until the mixture resembles breadcrumbs. Add the sugar. Spread over the fruit mixture.

Bake at 190°C/375°F (Gas 5) for 45–50 minutes or until the topping is browned. Serve hot with single cream or custard.

Vaccinium myrtillus

CRANBERRY

The deep red fruit of the cranberry is now probably best known in the form of cranberry sauce, traditionally served in America with the Thanksgiving turkey. The American cranberry is, in fact, larger than the British one and a Victorian Botanical Dictionary remarks that the French Canadians 'call it Atopa, a name they have borrowed from the Indians'. It is now cultivated in America, but although growing widely in the past in Britain, these days it is hard to find. The same book says: 'It is generally found entangled in Sphagnum and other bog-mosses, which cover the surface of shallow waters through which those who gather the fruit are obliged to wade. Being a native of bogs, it cannot be propagated upon dry land.' If you are lucky enough to find a quantity in marshy and boggy country, try the recipes below: if not, it is now easy to buy imported cranberries to use, even if it is cheating a little.

TRADITIONAL CRANBERRY MUFFINS
225 g (8 oz) plain flour
2.5 g (½ tsp) salt
75 g (3 oz) caster sugar
10 g (2 tsp) baking powder
2 large eggs
150 ml (¼ pt) milk
75 g (3 oz) butter
100 g (4 oz) fresh cranberries (coarsely chopped)
Grated rind of 1 orange

Butter some deep-holed patty tins (the mixture will make about 10 or 12 muffins). Preheat the oven to 220°C/400°F (Gas 6). Mix together the flour, salt, sugar and baking powder, then sift. Put the eggs into a bowl and beat in the milk a little at a time, then mix in the melted butter, cranberries and orange rind. Tip the flour in all at once and mix all together very quickly and lightly (it need not be very thoroughly mixed).

Fill the prepared tins about two-thirds full and bake in the centre of the oven for about 25 minutes until risen and browned. Serve buttered and very hot.

CRANBERRY SAUCE
This is a rich and delicious Victorian recipe.
600 ml (1 pt) cranberries
150 ml (¼ pt) water
50 g (2 oz) caster sugar
15 ml (1 tbsp) redcurrant jelly
30 ml (2 tbsp) port

Put the washed cranberries in a pan with the water and simmer gently for 30 minutes, then add the rest of the ingredients. Bring to the boil, skim and strain. May be served either hot or cold. (Alternatively, cook the cranberries for longer, until they are almost a pulp, add the other ingredients and bring to the boil again. Serve without straining).

RICH CRANBERRY FLAN

For the pastry:
175 g (6 oz) plain flour
100 g (4 oz) butter
25 g (1 oz) caster sugar
15 ml (1 tbsp) water

For the filling:
75 g (3 oz) raisins
75 g (3 oz) currants
50 g (2 oz) chopped mixed peel (or use 225 g (8 oz) ready mixed fruit with mixed peel)
50 g (2 oz) walnuts or hazelnuts, chopped
60 ml (4 tbsp) cranberry sauce (see recipe above)
25 g (1 oz) butter, melted
Icing sugar

Rub the butter into the flour, add the sugar and mix to a firm dough with the water.

Line a 20-cm (8-in) fluted flan tin with the rolled-out mixture, reserving any trimmings to form a lattice top or shape to decorate. Bake the flan case 'blind' at 200°C/400°F (Gas 6) for 25 minutes. Remove from oven. Mix all the other ingredients except the icing sugar and put in the flan case. Decorate top with pastry lattice then bake at 180°C/350°F (Gas 4) for a further 15–20 minutes. Take from the oven, cool a little then sprinkle top lightly with icing sugar. May be eaten warm or cold, with fresh cream.
Serves 6

CRANBERRY-STUFFED TURKEY

225 g (8 oz) finely chopped onion
100 g (4 oz) finely chopped celery
25 g (1 oz) butter
175 g (6 oz) breadcrumbs, toasted
Juice and rind of 1 orange
Juice and rind of $\frac{1}{2}$ lemon
5 tbsp cranberry sauce
Salt and pepper to taste
2 tsp dried thyme or mixed herbs
1 egg, beaten

This stuffing is sufficient for a 4.5 kg (10 lb) turkey.

Fry the onion and celery in the butter until soft, then add the crumbs, rind and juice of the orange and lemon, the cranberry sauce, salt and pepper and herbs. Bind with the beaten egg and stuff the bird.

For a really novel flavour, mix together a further 3 tablespoons of cranberry sauce with 50 g (2 oz) of butter seasoned with salt and pepper. With a sharp knife loosen the skin over the stuffed turkey breast and insert the cranberry butter in the space between the skin and breast. Secure the skin with fine skewers.

Dot the turkey with 50 g (2 oz) more butter and sprinkle with a little salt and pepper. Cover with the foil and roast at 190°C/375°F (Gas 5) for 25 minutes per lb (stuffed weight) plus an extra 25 minutes. Take off the foil for the last twenty minutes to brown the breast. Serve with the usual vegetable accompaniments, bacon rolls, chipolatas, bread sauce and gravy made from juices in the pan. Depending on appetite, serves 10–15!

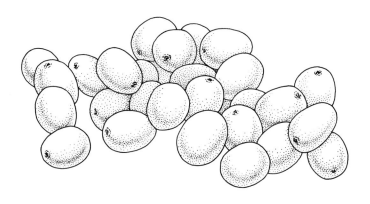

Viola odorata

SWEET VIOLET

'That which above all others yields the sweetest smell in the Aire is the Violet, specially the white-double-violet which comes twice a yeare; about the middle of Aprill and about Bartholomewtide.' I agree with Francis Bacon. One of the most memorable happenings on a country walk is to notice a delightful fragrance and try to find its source. It happened to me in a country lane in Wiltshire, and on looking over the hedge, there was a bank of sweet white violets in the full sunshine. The scent was so strong that I could smell it nearly a quarter of a mile away and it was certainly a bank which would have fitted Titania and all her court! You can find sweet violets in all shades from deep purple to white and any may be used in cooking. They were popular in Victorian times for delicate recipes, and crop up in literary quotations, from Shakespeare down. Both the flowers and leaves can be used. Candy the flowers in the same way as primroses.

VIOLET HONEY
300 ml (½ pt) water
50 g (2 oz) scented violet flowers
450 g (1 lb) honey

Boil the water and pour it over the violets. Stir well, and stand, covered, overnight. Press through a sieve to extract the liquid and add the honey to this. Boil together until thick and syrupy, then pour into jars and cover.

BROWN BREAD ICE CREAM WITH VIOLETS
300 ml (½ pt) double cream
15 ml (1 tbsp) brandy
75 g (3 oz) freshly-made brown breadcrumbs, dried in the oven
75 g (3 oz) coffee sugar crystals, lightly crushed
Crystallised violets (to make, see recipe for crystallised primroses)
6 violet chocolate creams, chilled and finely chopped

Whip the cream a little (it should not be too stiff) and stir in the breadcrumbs and brandy. Freeze until mushy, then stir in the sugar and violet chocolates and freeze again in a decorative mould. To serve, turn out and decorate all over with crystallised violets. This ice cream has an interesting crunchy texture.
Serves 4–6

PERFUMED WINE
1 bottle sweet white wine
Violet flowers

Pick the petals from a large bunch of violets and put them in the wine, leaving for seven or eight days. Remove the old petals and repeat with fresh petals. Strain, chill the wine which is now ready for drinking. Best, in my opinion, as an aperitif.

Viola odorata

Index